Text and Performance

General Editor: Michael Scott

The series is designed to introduce sixth-form and undergraduate students to the themes, continuing vitality and performance of major dramatic works. The attention given to production aspects is an element of special importance, responding to the invigoration given to literary study by the work of leading contemporary critics.

The prime aim is to present each play as a vital experience in the mind of the reader – achieved by analysis of the text in relation to its themes and theatricality. Emphasis is accordingly placed on the relevance of the work to the modern reader and the world of today. At the same time, traditional views are presented and appraised, forming the basis from which a creative response to the text can develop.

In each volume, Part One: *Text* discusses certain key themes or problems, the reader being encouraged to gain a stronger perception both of the inherent character of the work and also of variations in interpreting it. Part Two: *Performance* examines the ways in which these themes or problems have been handled in modern productions, and the approaches and techniques employed to enhance the play's accessibility to modern audiences.

A Synopsis of the play is given and an outline of its major sources, and a concluding Reading List offers guidance to the student's independent study of the work.

A MIDSUMMER NIGHT'S DREAM

Text and Performance

ROGER WARREN

First published 1983 by
THE MACMILLAN PRESS LTD
Companies and representatives
throughout the world

ISBN 0 333 33998 3 (pbk)

Typeset by
WESSEX TYPESETTERS LTD,
Frome, Somerset
Printed in Hong Kong

CONTENTS

Illustrations will be found in Part Two.

ACKNOWLEDGEMENTS

Quotations from *A Midsummer Night's Dream* are from the New Penguin Shakespeare edition (1967), edited by Stanley Wells.

Other quotations from Shakespeare are from *The Complete Works* (1951), edited by Peter Alexander.

All quotations, except those from Chaucer, are given in modern spelling.

Source-details for the illustrations are given with the relevant captions to the plates.

GENERAL EDITOR'S PREFACE

For many years a mutual suspicion existed between the theatre director and the literary critic of drama. Although in the first half of the century there were important exceptions, such was the rule. A radical change of attitude, however, has taken place over the last thirty years. Critics and directors now increasingly recognise the significance of each other's work and acknowledge their growing awareness of interdependence. Both interpret the same text, but do so according to their different situations and functions. Without the director, the designer and the actor, a play's existence is only partial. They revitalise the text with action, enabling the drama to live fully at each performance. The academic critic investigates the script to elucidate its textual problems, understand its conventions and discover how it operates. He may also propose his view of the work, expounding what he considers to be its significance.

Dramatic texts belong therefore to theatre and to literature. The aim of the 'Text and Performance' series is to achieve a fuller recognition of how both enhance our enjoyment of the play. Each volume follows the same basic pattern. Part One provides a critical introduction to the play under discussion, using the techniques and criteria of the literary critic in examining the manner in which the work operates through language, imagery and action. Part Two takes the enquiry further into the play's theatricality by focusing on selected productions of recent times so as to illustrate points of contrast and comparison in the interpretation of different directors and actors, and to demonstrate how the drama has worked on the modern stage. In this way the series seeks to provide a lively and informative introduction to major plays in their text and performance.

MICHAEL SCOTT

PLOT SYNOPSIS AND SOURCES

Theseus, Duke of Athens, is about to marry his former enemy Hippolyta, Queen of the Amazons. Bottom and other local workmen plan to perform a play for the royal wedding day. On that day, too, Hermia must reply to her father Egeus's demand that she should marry Demetrius, whom he favours, rather than Lysander, whom she loves. Hermia and Lysander decide to meet in the nearby wood, and flee from Athens. They are followed to the wood by Demetrius, and by Helena, whom he had loved before he met Hermia.

In the wood, Oberon, King of the fairies, is quarrelling with his Queen, Titania, because she will not give him a little changeling boy to be his page. In revenge, Oberon anoints her eyes with the juice of a magic flower which has the power to make her fall in love with the next creature that she sees. The workmen come to the wood to rehearse their play. Oberon's servant Puck puts an ass's head upon Bottom, and Titania falls in love with him in this form.

Oberon instructs Puck to use the magic flower to restore Demetrius's love for Helena. Puck mistakes Lysander for Demetrius, with the result that both men now pursue Helena, rather than Hermia. Much confusion and a prolonged quarrel follow. Eventually, Oberon intervenes and restores the four lovers to their original partners.

Under the spell of her infatuation with Bottom, Titania agrees to give Oberon the changeling boy. Oberon frees her from the spell, and they are reconciled. Theseus over-rides Egeus's objections, and the three couples are married. At their wedding celebrations, Bottom and his friends perform their play. Finally, the fairies come from the wood to bless the palace and the three marriages.

Sources

There is no major source for *A Midsummer Night's Dream*, but Shakespeare probably drew on Chaucer's *The Knight's Tale* and North's translation of Plutarch's *Lives of the Noble Grecians and Romans* for Theseus, Ovid's *Metamorphoses* for the story of Pyramus and Thisbe, Apuleius's *The Golden Ass* for Bottom's transformation and the old romance *Huon of Bordeaux* and folklore for the fairies.

PART ONE: TEXT

1 INTRODUCTION

Ill met by moonlight, proud Titania!

Few characters in Shakespeare have such an arresting opening line as this. Oberon and Titania are no sooner on stage than they are in the throes of a fierce domestic quarrel. If the audience has any preconceptions about fairies being remote or ethereal or insipid, the vigorous opening phrases of these particular fairies should quickly banish any such expectations: 'What, *jealous* Oberon', 'I have *forsworn* his bed', 'Tarry, *rash wanton!*' [II i 60–3]. They accuse each other of having affairs with the other royal couple in the play, Theseus and Hippolyta. Like many quarrelling husbands and wives, they do not hesitate to parody the characteristics of their rivals. Titania mocks the way that Oberon's 'buskined mistress' Hippolyta walks, 'bouncing' in her hunting boots; and Oberon counters that by accusing her of causing Theseus to abandon his various other mistresses [II i 70–80]. This fairy king and queen are immediately established as powerful dramatic characters who have both human passions and more than human influence over the affections of other people.

The dramatic vigour of this fairy quarrel requires emphasis at the outset, because much influential modern criticism does not take the fairies at face value, as characters in a play, but as a metaphor for something quite different. C. L. Barber, for instance, says that 'producers utterly ruin the scene when they have the fairy couple mouth their lines at each other as expressively as possible' (*Shakespeare's Festive Comedy*, 1959, p. 147). It is difficult to see how actors could possibly avoid being expressive when speaking the lines quoted above, but Barber's argument is that 'we are not asked to think that fairies exist'. Instead, they represent 'a creative tendency and process'

(p. 162). This process is, as D. J. Palmer puts it in his survey of current criticism of the play, 'the transforming power of the imagination, which most critics regard as its central preoccupation' ('The Early Comedies', *Shakespeare: Select Bibliographical Guides*, ed. Stanley Wells, 1973, p. 65).

The fullest statement of this point of view is David P. Young's book *Something of Great Constancy* (1966). He accurately describes the great variety of poetic styles within the play, but instead of exploring the dramatic effects of what he calls 'stylistic shifts', he claims that 'these lead us in turn to more abstract sets of opposites like illusion and reality or . . . art versus nature' (p. 67). He even suggests that many of the long poetic speeches cannot be justified in dramatic terms because they are 'elaborated beyond the dramatic requirements of a given situation' (p. 5). He thinks however that they can be justified in thematic terms: 'in their evocation of the imagination, their illustration of its follies, triumphs, and possibilities, they realize the play's basic theme' (pp. 75–6). The difficulty here is that the poetic speeches themselves are so much more interesting than the 'theme' which they are supposed to represent. The suggestion that 'the richness of interest of *A Midsummer Night's Dream* lies, in large part, in its expression of contemporaneous intellectual issues' (p. 113) seems to me actually to reduce both the richness and the interest, since it substitutes 'abstract sets of opposites', like imagination and reason or art and nature, for the theatrical life of Shakespeare's play. It is hard to imagine any audience responding to *A Midsummer Night's Dream* in this way.

Far from being 'elaborated beyond the dramatic requirements', the extended lyrical speeches of the fairies, in particular, are the very effective dramatic means by which Shakespeare creates their world. The point is made in an admirably concise account of the play by G. K. Hunter:

in the case of the fairies Shakespeare is to be credited with the creation, single-handed, of an entirely new world. What the play required was a world which was both benevolent and mysterious . . . ; the natural beauties of the moonlit wood are sumptuously described in order to evoke the spirits who dwell among them.

(*Shakespeare: The Later Comedies*, 1962, p. 15.)

He does not ignore the topic of imagination, which after all Theseus and Hippolyta themselves discuss in the play scene, but he does not force it into becoming the 'basic theme' either:

> Was the adventure of the lovers true or false, real or imaginary? The play would seem to answer, 'both true and false'. For Theseus it is false, for Theseus lives in a rational daylight world where, as for any good ruler, things have to be defined before they can be accepted. But the lovers can live in the result of their 'dream' without worrying about the status of its truth.   (p. 19)

The advantage of such criticism is that it concentrates upon the dramatic facts. I have attempted to do this in my own account, which approaches *A Midsummer Night's Dream* by way of its four-part structure, focusing attention on the dramatic technique with which Shakespeare characterises four distinct worlds (the court, the fairies, the lovers, and the mechanicals) and on the various ways in which he brings them together. In short, it attempts to describe how the play works as a play.

Although the exact date is uncertain, *A Midsummer Night's Dream* was probably written in 1594/95. It is, therefore, one of Shakespeare's earlier plays, but already he shows absolute confidence in handling both language and structure, to very clear dramatic ends. Peter Hall, who has often directed the play, points out that its lyrical beauty 'is not sentimental. It's about the actuality of passion, of natural life. . . . These comedies . . . are all about sex, the pain of sex, the difficulty of it, and the essential desire on everybody's part to achieve love' (*Sunday Times*, 14 June 1981). Shakespeare dramatises many different aspects of love and marriage, not only in the course of creating the individual groups of characters, but also in the way he combines them. The wedding celebration of the former adversaries Theseus and Hippolyta is the event towards which the four plots move, and which finally unites all four groups of characters in the last scene. Both Theseus's ironical view of love, and the mechanicals' play about star-crossed lovers, place the extravagance of the four young lovers in perspective. While the courtiers and the lovers move towards marriage, the fairy quarrel shows one of its consequences, a powerful image of marital discord. By giving the fairies the power to influence the love of mortals, Shakespeare can dramatise the irrational nature of love by means of the stage action itself. When Oberon and Puck squeeze the juice of the magic flower into people's eyes, this is a very effective image of the arbitrariness of human attraction – how people may be, quite literally, 'smitten' with love.

David P. Young usefully summarises the different kinds of style which are associated with the different groups of characters: 'although the usage is by no means strict, we associate blank verse with Theseus, Hippolyta, and the courtly world . . . ; couplets with the lovers . . . ; lyrical measures . . . with the fairy world; and prose with the mechanicals.' (*Something of Great Constancy*, p. 66.) Shakespeare handles these various styles with equal fluency. All the language in this play is notable for its ease and clarity. There is a good example of this at the very beginning, when Hippolyta assures Theseus that the four days before their wedding will quickly pass:

> And then the moon – like to a silver bow
> New-bent in heaven – shall behold the night
> Of our solemnities.   [i i 9–11]

The comparison of the new moon to a bow bent to shoot is not insisted upon; the phrase does a great deal of work with very little effort. It is appropriate for Hippolyta, an Amazonian huntress, to liken the crescent moon to a bent bow; it picks up Theseus's impatient 'how slow / This old moon wanes' in his opening speech [i i 3–4]; and it anticipates the play's many references to the moon, by whose light important events will be acted out in the wood. Perhaps, too, the tension required to bend a bow hints that she is as impatient as Theseus for their wedding night. But none of these points is laboured. The chief quality of Hippolyta's speech is its easy flow. Like all good writing for the stage, it communicates the sense without drawing undue attention to itself.

One feature of the language requires particular emphasis, since it contributes more than anything else to the play's individual flavour. In many of his plays and poems, Shakespeare seems to turn spontaneously to the English countryside for comparisons which will express his meaning as immediately and effectively as possible, especially when he is writing about love. In *Love's Labour's Lost*, for instance, he makes Berowne express the tenderness of a lover's feelings by appealing to something tender and vulnerable from the natural world:

> Love's feeling is more soft and sensible
> Than are the tender horns of cockled snails. [*L.L.L.*, iv iii 333–4]

Such language is especially characteristic of *A Midsummer Night's Dream*. In the first scene, Helena says to Hermia,

> Your eyes are lodestars, and your tongue's sweet air
> More tuneable than lark to shepherd's ear
> When wheat is green, when hawthorn buds appear.   [i i 183–5]

The images here beautifully express Helena's bitter-sweet experience of seeing her lover lured away by the superior charms of her best friend: just as lodestars guide travellers, so Hermia's eyes have drawn Demetrius away from Helena, and Hermia's voice has enchanted him as a lark's song delights a shepherd in springtime. Shakespeare uses vivid poetic evocations of the countryside for two other closely related dramatic purposes: to suggest the wood itself, in a theatre which had little or no scenery, and to characterise the fairies who inhabit it.

2   THE FAIRIES

In their opening quarrel, Shakespeare makes Oberon and Titania immediately striking characters by giving them human passions; but he also needs to differentiate them from human beings, without losing that sense of tangible reality. As Peter Hall puts it, 'fairy tales must be concrete if they are to be human and not whimsical' (*Sunday Times*, 26 Jan. 1969). Shakespeare achieves this by presenting them in terms of the natural world in which they live, evoked in concrete detail: the loveliest, most delicate wild flowers, the sunrise over the sea – and also frost, rain, and mud. Shakespeare varies the image he presents of the countryside in order to reflect different aspects of the fairies themselves. This can be demonstrated by considering four passages in detail, first Titania's account of the chaotic weather which has resulted from her quarrel with Oberon [II i 81–117], and then three of Oberon's major speeches: his description of Titania's bower [II i 249–56], his evocation of the sunrise [III ii 388–93], and his vision which introduces the magic flower [II i 148–68]. Each of these passages is placed at a dramatically important moment in the play. Each helps to characterise the fairies and their world, and to establish what kind of spirits they are.

In Titania's long speech about the bad weather, Shakespeare differentiates her from the mortals by associating her very directly with the countryside, which she describes in both general and specific terms. At the same time, he never loses sight of the particular dramatic situation. This speech is Titania's most extensive accusation of Oberon during their quarrel. She begins angrily as she dismisses Oberon's accusations:

> These are the forgeries of jealousy;
> And never   . . .

But then both mood and tempo change. With the phrase 'the middle summer's spring', Titania slows the line down as her mind begins to range over the natural world, and to create it verbally for the audience:

> . . .   since the middle summer's spring
> Met we on hill, in dale, forest, or mead,
> By pavèd fountain or by rushy brook,
> Or in the beachèd margent of the sea
> To dance our ringlets to the whistling wind,
> But with thy brawls thou has disturbed our sport.   [II i 81–7]

That last line returns to the tense dramatic situation; but in the meantime Titania has told us a great deal about her world. Keats makes some illuminating comments on the implications of that phrase 'the middle summer's spring': 'There is something exquisitely rich and luxurious in Titania's saying "since the middle summer's spring" as if bowers were not exuberant and covert enough for fairy sports until their second sprouting. . . . The thing is a piece of profound verdure.' (Quoted in Caroline Spurgeon, *Keats's Shakespeare*, 1928, p. 52.)

Keats catches quite marvellously the mood of the first part of Titania's speech, that sense of an 'exuberant', 'sprouting' natural world in which the fairies live. As Titania evokes hill, dale, forest, mead, paved fountain, rushy brook, these become more than a mere background for the fairies; their whole way of life seems inseparably bound up with their surroundings. This relationship is a reciprocal one. Oberon's speeches later make it clear that the natural world is the source of their power; but at the same time it is under their influence, as Titania goes on to demonstrate.

The seasons themselves have been upset because of Titania's quarrel with Oberon, and the countryside has been plunged into exceptionally bad weather:

> Therefore the winds, piping to us in vain,
> As in revenge have sucked up from the sea
> Contagious fogs which, falling in the land,
> Hath every pelting river made so proud
> That they have overborne their continents.   [II i 88–92]

In this speech Shakespeare was probably drawing on the appalling weather of 1594, when the rivers indeed 'overbore their continents' and washed bridges away. The severity of this weather provoked much comment, for example from the astrologer Simon Forman:

> These months of June and July were very wet and wonderful cold like winter, that the tenth day of July many did sit by the fire, it was so cold; and so was it in May and June; and scarce two fair days together all that time.
> (Quoted in H. H. Furness's Variorum *Dream*, 1895, p. 252.)

It all sounds very familiar; and that is the point. Shakespeare did not draw on contemporary weather conditions simply to provide a forty-line topical allusion, but for a dramatic purpose which works just as well for us today. The speech appeals to an

audience's familiar experience of bad English summer weather:
Titania and her situation seem real and immediate, because
they are so closely related to ordinary human experience. To
intensify that experience, Titania moves from the general to the
very specific as she describes the miseries of the rural world in
detail:

> The ox hath therefore stretched his yoke in vain,
> The ploughman lost his sweat, and the green corn
> Hath rotted ere his youth attained a beard.
> . . .
> The nine men's morris is filled up with mud.   [ii i 93–8]

This fairy queen, far from being remotely ethereal, expresses
herself in terms of everyday country experience, even in terms
of a rural game whose playing area, cut out of the turf, is now
waterlogged. This image is the most extreme example of the
lengths to which Shakespeare goes to make these fairies
immediate.

The specific references to the nine men's morris and the
sweating ploughman also help to make clear Titania's point of
view. While she attacks Oberon for the effect their quarrel has
had on the human inhabitants of the countryside, she sym-
pathises with the mortal victims themselves, not only for the
wretched weather they have been enduring, but also for their
lack of any compensating pastimes:

> The human mortals want their winter cheer.
> No night is now with hymn or carol blessed.   [ii i 101–2]

This miserable picture of winter-in-summer leads her on to
describe the freak weather in a graphic personification of icy
winter (Hiems) wearing a coronet of summer buds:

> The seasons alter; hoary-headed frosts
> Fall in the fresh lap of the crimson rose,
> And on old Hiems' thin and icy crown
> An odorous chaplet of sweet summer buds
> Is as in mockery set.   [ii i 107–11]

The climax of Titania's speech is a general confusion of the
seasons:

> The spring, the summer,
> The childing autumn, angry winter change
> Their wonted liveries, and the mazèd world
> By their increase now knows not which is which.   [II i 111–14]

She concludes the speech as she began it, by returning to their quarrel which has caused all this chaos. It is all their fault:

> And this same progeny of evils
> Comes from our debate, from our dissension.
> We are their parents and original.   [II i 115–17]

Titania's concern for the 'human mortals' recurs in her next speech, where she explains that she refuses to give Oberon the changeling boy, and so end their quarrel, out of loyalty to his dead mother, 'a votaress of my order':

> But she, being mortal, of that boy did die,
> And for her sake do I rear up her boy;
> And for her sake I will not part with him.   [II i 135–7]

The sympathy which Titania expresses for mortals who are dependent on her is important, because it represents a departure from much Elizabethan literature and folklore, in which fairies were sinister creatures who misled hapless mortals and stole babies from their cradles. Shakespeare himself refers to this tradition in other plays. In *Hamlet*, fairies are associated with witches [I i 163]; in *Cymbeline*, Imogen prays for protection from 'fairies and the tempters of the night' [II ii 9]; and in *The Merry Wives of Windsor*, Falstaff refers to the popular superstition that 'he that speaks to them shall die' [v v 45].

The fairies of *A Midsummer Night's Dream* are not like this at all. Titania did not steal the changeling boy from his mortal mother; on the contrary, she loves and cherishes him for his mother's sake, even at the cost of a violent quarrel with Oberon. While, of course, the indirect result of this quarrel is unfortunate for the mortals because it inflicts a wretched summer upon them, the fairies' direct dealings with the mortals are benevolent. Although something of the traditional dangerous fairies survives in Puck's enjoyment of misleading the mechanicals and the lovers ('this their jangling I esteem a sport' [III ii 353]), even he is mischievous rather than malevolent: 'those things do best please me / That befall preposterously' [III ii 120–1]. And however mixed Puck's motives may be, Oberon's reason for intervening in the affairs of the lovers is sympathetic and entirely benevolent:

> Fare thee well, nymph. Ere he do leave this grove
> Thou shalt fly him, and he shall seek thy love.   [II i 245–6]

In making Oberon and Titania essentially benevolent towards mortals, Shakespeare was significantly modifying a tradition which he accepted in other plays.

Whereas Titania's speech about the bad weather expresses the disastrous consequences of the fairies' quarrel by creating a vivid picture of the unpleasant features of the natural world, three important speeches by Oberon evoke the wholesome and desirable beauty of the countryside to suggest the fairies' positive aspects and the source of their power. A very clear example is Oberon's description of Titania's bower,

> a bank where the wild thyme blows,
> Where oxlips and the nodding violet grows,
> Quite overcanopied with luscious woodbine,
> With sweet muskroses and with eglantine.   [II i 249–52]

This speech is more than a piece of verbal scene-painting. The bank seems to take on a life of its own. The language insists on the positive qualities of the natural world. In particular, the adjectives are carefully chosen to suggest delicacy ('*nodding* violet'), richness ('*luscious* woodbine') and attractiveness ('*sweet* muskroses'). The wild thyme 'blows' fragrance into the air; 'quite overcanopied' suggests a sense of security for Titania as she sleeps. The dramatic effect of the passage as a whole is to associate Titania herself with the positive beauty of her surroundings.

This connection between the beauty of the natural world and the fairies is emphasised even more strongly in Oberon's remarkable speech at the crucial dramatic moment, the turning-point of the play, when he intervenes to restore the lovers to their original partners. If these relationships are to seem lasting and genuine, it is dramatically essential that they should be clearly the work of a benevolent agency. There must be no hint that Oberon's power might derive from black magic or evil spirits; so Shakespeare conclusively banishes any such possibility in an especially striking way. He begins by actually making Puck describe, in considerable detail, those malevolent spirits with whom fairies were often associated in popular folk tradition:

> My fairy lord, this must be done with haste,
> For night's swift dragons cut the clouds full fast,
> And yonder shines Aurora's harbinger,
> At whose approach ghosts wandering here and there
> Troop home to churchyards. Damnèd spirits all
> That in crossways and floods have burial
> Already to their wormy beds are gone.
> For fear lest day should look their shames upon
> They wilfully themselves exile from light,
> And must for aye consort with black-browed night.   [III ii 378–87]

In terms of the narrative, it is quite unnecessary for Puck to mention these evil spirits at all, let alone at such length; all he needs to do for the immediate requirements of the scene (especially since he has urged haste) is to announce the dawn as briefly as he does in the next scene: 'Fairy king, attend, and mark: / I do hear the morning lark' [IV i 92–3]. Shakespeare goes out of his way to remind the audience of malevolent spirits so that he can then dispose once and for all of the possibility that his own fairies might be of this kind, by making Oberon specifically dissociate himself and his realm from them:

> But *we* are spirits of another sort.

Although Shakespeare gives Oberon this categorical denial of malevolence, he obviously feels that it is not enough to make the point negatively, and so he goes on to suggest a very positive source for Oberon's power:

> I with the morning's love have oft made sport,
> And like a forester the groves may tread
> Even till the eastern gate all fiery red

Opening on Neptune with fair blessèd beams
Turns into yellow gold his salt green streams.   [III ii 388–93]

The last three lines are an evocation of the sunrise over the sea:
so, whereas the fairies are associated elsewhere with trees,
flowers, fountains, brooks, and so on, Shakespeare now associates Oberon with the sunrise, with the source of light itself, with
the warmth and health of the *fair blessèd* beams' of the sun. The
basic dramatic point made by the speech is that Oberon is a
spirit of light, not a spirit of darkness like those Puck has just
described.

But what precisely does Oberon mean by the striking phrase
'I with the morning's love have oft made sport'? It has been
suggested that, since Oberon immediately goes on to say 'And
like a forester the groves may tread', he means that he has gone
hunting ('made sport' in that sense) with the huntsman
Cephalus, who in classical myth was loved by Aurora, the
goddess of the dawn (and so 'the morning's love'). The
Cephalus story was certainly running in Shakespeare's head
while he was writing the *Dream*, for he refers to it in the play
scene where Bottom characteristically mispronounces the
names of both Cephalus and his wife Procris – 'not Shafalus to
Procrus was so true' [v i 195] – and it is almost certain that this
story was the starting-point for the image of Oberon as a
forester in the woods at sunrise. 'I with the morning's love have
oft made sport', however, implies something much stronger
than that Oberon went hunting in the company of the morning's lover. 'Made sport' suggests, not hunting, but sexual
dalliance. The evocative image of a figure sporting with, being
enveloped by, the 'fair blessèd beams' of the rising sun implies
that Oberon has made love with the goddess of the dawn
herself; or, more impressionistically, has made love with the
sunrise itself. What Shakespeare seems to have done here is to
have taken the figure of a mythological forester in the dawn
woods beloved by the goddess of the morning, but changed the
figure from Cephalus to Oberon himself, so that 'I with the
morning's love have oft made sport' could be paraphrased 'I
have dallied with the love of the morning itself [herself]'. This
develops into the magnificent image of the sun rising over the
sea and turning its waves into gold. The dramatic effect of the

whole speech is to give a graphic impression of Oberon in particular and the fairies in general as benevolent agents who derive their power from potent natural sources.

Shakespeare's technique here of transforming an existing myth into a new one occurs at another important dramatic moment when Oberon sends Puck to fetch the little western flower with which he can make people fall in love. As in the sunrise speech, Oberon makes it clear once again that he derives his power from the natural world, since 'love-in-idleness' is a rural nickname for the pansy. In view of the importance of this theatrical property to the action of the play as a whole, Shakespeare needs to focus considerable attention on the flower from the first moment it is mentioned. He does this by transforming another kind of myth for his own dramatic purposes: he combines the rural world of which the flower is a part with the formal world of Queen Elizabeth I's court, by introducing a vision of the Queen herself. This is the most emphatic of a number of allusions to the Queen in the play. The hierarchy of the fairy court is based on Elizabeth's own, with Puck as court jester ('I jest to Oberon, and make him smile' [II i 44]); the cowslips in the wood are Titania's equivalent of Elizabeth's 'pensioners' or personal bodyguard of young courtiers [II i 10]; and Titania's name is taken from Ovid's *Metamorphoses* (iii 173), where it is a synonym for Diana, one of the mythological names most frequently used to compliment Elizabeth herself. The ritual of her court had transformed the Queen's reluctance to marry into a divine quality, glorifying her as the earthly embodiment of Diana, the goddess of chastity. It is this aspect of the courtly cult of the Virgin Queen that Shakespeare takes as his starting-point for the imaginative speech which introduces the dramatically crucial flower.

Oberon recalls an occasion when Cupid aimed his arrow, which has the power to inflame its victim with love, at a 'fair vestal thronèd by the west'. This is a clear reference to the Queen. Cupid

> loosed his loveshaft smartly from his bow
> As it should pierce a hundred thousand hearts;
> But I might see young Cupid's fiery shaft
> Quenched in the chaste beams of the watery moon,

And the imperial votaress passed on
In maiden meditation, fancy-free.   [ii i 158–64]

The dramatic point of the speech is that when Cupid's arrow
could make no impact on the Virgin Queen, it fell upon the
little western flower. This explains how the flower has acquired
the power to make people fall in love. The speech is an unmistakable allusion to Elizabeth surviving a love-suit; and Oberon
introduces it with a reminiscence of what sounds like a specific
occasion. 'Thou rememberest', he says to Puck,

Since once I sat upon a promontory
And heard a mermaid on a dolphin's back
Uttering such dulcet and harmonious breath
That the rude sea grew civil at her song,
And certain stars shot madly from their spheres
To hear the sea-maid's music?   [ii i 148–54]

Various court occasions have been mentioned in connection
with this speech. The closest resemblances to Oberon's vision
occurred in a great Warwickshire event held only thirteen miles
from Stratford when Shakespeare was eleven. This was the
elaborate three-week entertainment known as the 'Princely
Pleasures' which Elizabeth's favourite Robert Dudley, Earl of
Leicester, lavished upon the Queen at Kenilworth Castle in
1575, of which we have a detailed contemporary account by
Robert Laneham (reprinted as a Scolar Press Facsimile, 1968).
A typical example of the entertainments on that occasion was
an elaborate water-pageant, including, says Laneham, 'a
swimming mermaid (that from top to tail was an eighteen foot
long)' and Arion 'riding aloft upon his old friend the dolphin,
that from head to tail was a four and twenty foot long'. It was
obviously quite a spectacle; and these two striking figures seem
fused into one in Oberon's line 'a mermaid on a dolphin's
back'. In both cases the figure riding on the dolphin is singing
sweetly: Oberon says that the mermaid uttered 'dulcet and
harmonious breath', Laneham that Arion 'began a delectable
ditty of a song well apted to a melodious noise, compounded of
six several instruments . . . casting sound from the dolphin's
belly within' (pp. 40–3). Leicester also entertained Elizabeth
with firework displays, 'with blaze of burning darts, flying to

and fro, . . . stars coruscant, streams and hail of fiery sparks, . . . that . . . the waters surged' in the lake (p. 16). Oberon's speech seems to combine this spectacle with the water-pageant:

> the rude sea grew civil at her song,
> And certain stars shot madly from their spheres
> To hear the sea-maid's music.

As for the love-suit clearly suggested by Cupid shooting at Elizabeth, George Gascoigne in his account of the Princely Pleasures (1576, reprinted 1587) describes a pageant in which Leicester himself is thinly disguised in the allegorical character of 'Deepdesire' who addressed the Queen from a holly-bush:

> Vouchsafe, O comely Queen, yet longer to remain,
> Or still to dwell amongst us here! O Queen, command again
> This Castle and the Knight, which keeps the same for you;
> . . .
> Live here, good Queen, live here.
>   (J. Nichols, *The Progresses of Queen Elizabeth*, 1823, p. 522.)

But despite this publicly-conducted wooing, the Queen departed 'in maiden meditation, fancy-free'.

Oberon's vision is so familiar that it is worth emphasising just how surprising its details are. A singing mermaid on a dolphin, accompanied by shooting stars, is not the most obvious thing to invent in order to introduce a magic flower; but if Shakespeare was thinking about the folklore and countryside of his native Warwickshire in order to create the rural aspect of the fairy world, this celebrated Warwickshire court occasion may well have seemed a suitable starting-point for Oberon's vision of Elizabeth's resistance to Cupid's power. If so, as with Shakespeare's probable re-working of the Cephalus myth in Oberon's sunrise speech, he has transformed it, reshaping and combining various aspects of the entertainments to create another new myth in order to explain how the little western flower came to have the power of bestowing love. Whether or not Shakespeare is transforming memories of this particular court spectacle, he is certainly drawing on the general mythology and pageantry of Elizabeth's court and

combining it with the immediacy of the countryside to create
the special world of the fairies, which is therefore 'Elizabethan'
in a specific sense. It is significant that of the four modern
directors whose productions are discussed in Part Two, Peter
Hall and Robin Phillips obviously felt that the atmosphere of
an Elizabethan court was essential to the play; and Elijah
Moshinsky, while setting it somewhat later, recognised its
affiliations to court entertainments by basing elements of his
version on the court masque. All three productions thereby
provided an appropriate visual equivalent not only for the fairy
kingdom but for Theseus's court as well.

3 THE COURT

Peter Hall succinctly characterises the essential features of
Shakespeare's portrait of Theseus and his court:

> Shakespeare's play is set in Athens. But this classical device is to
> distance and romanticise what is, in fact, a very Elizabethan and
> very English play. . . . Theseus is no pagan warrior, but a country
> Duke who practises an essentially English brand of pragmatism
> when things get difficult.
>
> (*Sunday Times*, 26 Jan. 1969.)

The reference to 'a *country* Duke' emphasises that Shakespeare
again brings together the court and the countryside, as in the
fairy world, but with significant differences, so that Oberon's
and Theseus's courts are connected and contrasted.

Both the resemblances and the differences are clearest in IV i,
one of the play's major transitions from one world to another.
There is a striking dramatic contrast between the fairies' dance
of 'amity' and the sound of the hunting horns which heralds the
daylight brilliance of Theseus's hunting party, arriving in the
dawn light ('the vaward of the day'). There is a corresponding
verbal contrast. On the one hand, the fairies speak formal
couplets as they dance:

Sound, music! Come, my Queen, take hands with me,
And rock the ground whereon these sleepers be.
Now thou and I are new in amity,
And will tomorrow midnight solemnly
Dance in Duke Theseus' house triumphantly,
And bless it to all fair prosperity.   [IV i 84–9]

On the other hand, as Theseus enters, he issues brisk instructions to 'find out the forester' and unleash the dogs:

Uncouple in the western valley; let them go.
Dispatch, I say, and find the forester.   [IV i 102–7]

There are connections, too, between the two worlds. Patrick Stewart, who played Oberon in John Barton's 1977 Stratford production, suggests an interesting link between Theseus's repeated instructions about finding the forester, and Oberon's speech discussed earlier about walking through the woods at sunrise 'like a forester':

There's so much that [Shakespeare] could have selected and he chooses 'forester' where a scene and a half earlier Oberon has . . . described himself as being a forester in the wood. And one gets a shimmering sense of these two figures, Theseus and Oberon, having contact in the forest – that there has been a time when Oberon, as a forester, has met and associated with Theseus.

(*Shakespeare Superscribe*, ed. Myra Barrs, 1980, p. 99.)

The connection which Patrick Stewart suggests here between Oberon as a forester and Theseus would reinforce the other connections made between the two pairs of rulers during the fairy quarrel, when Oberon and Titania accuse each other of having had affairs in the past with Theseus and Hippolyta respectively. It could be suggested simply and effectively in performance. There is no break between Oberon's exit and Theseus's entry at IV i 101. If, as Theseus appears, he catches a glimpse of Oberon disappearing, he could make both his references to the forester apply to the figure he saw departing. To connect the two figures for a fleeting moment as the 'glimmering night' gives way to the 'shimmering' dawn would emphasise how Shakespeare contrasts yet relates the two worlds.

G. K. Hunter valuably points out that 'the image of Theseus and Hippolyta is a magnetic one, built up with a marvellous economy of means' (*Shakespeare: The Later Comedies*, p. 18). An excellent example of this economy is Hippolyta's casual line about how she took part in a memorable hunt 'with Hercules and Cadmus once' [IV i 111]. Hercules was Theseus's kinsman, and is referred to as such at V i 47, but Cadmus, the founder of Thebes, belonged to a much earlier period of classical legend. Hercules and Cadmus could not, therefore, have gone hunting together. There was no such legendary hunt. Shakespeare has made it up. This is another example of the way in which classical figures act primarily as a stimulus for Shakespeare's own imagination. Just as he seems to have transformed the story of Cephalus and Aurora into that evocative picture of Oberon making love with the sunrise, so here the association of Theseus and Hippolyta with Hercules and Cadmus lends a touch of exotic grandeur to their hunting speeches.

Those speeches themselves serve several other dramatic purposes. Hippolyta's account of Hercules's hunt does not merely refer to the past, but helps to make the stage action itself more immediate: it is a way of giving the audience the sensation of actually being in a wood which is so echoing with barking dogs and horn calls that it seems 'all one mutual cry' [IV i 116]. This is achieved, of course, primarily by sound, both in the use of the hunting horns themselves, and in the verbal details, which suggest a kind of rural music, what Theseus calls 'the musical confusion / Of hounds and echo in conjunction' [IV i 109–10]. Hippolyta's speech, like Titania's account of the bad weather, lists features of the countryside to give a sense of the extensive range of the wood itself:

> Never did I hear
> Such gallant chiding, for besides the groves,
> The skies, the fountains, every region near
> Seemed all one mutual cry. I never heard
> So musical a discord, such sweet thunder.   [IV i 113–17]

'Such *sweet* thunder': as in Oberon's phrase about the 'sweet muskroses' on Titania's bower, the countryside is not described with cold objectivity, but with affection. 'Sweet thunder' perfectly catches Hippolyta's enthusiasm for the musical quality of the hunt. This enthusiasm is a particularly Elizabethan one. It has the same relish, for instance, as the account (mentioned earlier) by Robert Laneham of a hunt in which Queen Elizabeth participated during her visit to Kenilworth Castle in 1575. Laneham insists particularly, like Hippolyta, on the way that the sounds of the hunt were enhanced by exceptional echoes. In the woods around the Castle,

> the earning of the hounds in continuance of their cry, . . . the blasting of horns, the halloing and hewing of the huntsmen, with the excellent echoes between whiles from the woods and waters in valleys resounding, moved pastime delectable in so high a degree [that] there can be none any way comparable to this: and special in this place, that of nature is formed so feet for the purpose.
> (*A Letter* . . ., 1575; Scolar Press Facsimile, 1968, pp. 17–18.)

The main dramatic purpose of the hunting scene is to establish Theseus, Hippolyta and their world in terms of the rural pursuits of an Elizabethan court, so that they have the immediacy and reality of two Elizabethan aristocrats.

The details of the hunt also enable Shakespeare to sharpen his characterisation of Theseus, who responds to Hippolyta's description of the musical quality of the 'hounds of Sparta' during Hercules's hunt [IV i 113] by expressing enthusiasm about his own dogs, which he considers fully equal to those of his 'kinsman, Hercules':

> My hounds are bred out of the Spartan kind;
> So flewed, so sanded; and their heads are hung
> With ears that sweep away the morning dew;
> Crook-kneed; and dewlapped like Thessalian bulls. [IV i 118–21]

In the next line, however, his enthusiastic tone takes an unexpected turn, as he admits that the dogs have what looks like a serious defect: they are 'slow in pursuit'. Then he reverts to his former enthusiasm as he suggests that this is compensated for by the same quality of sound that Hippolyta so admired in Crete:

> Slow in pursuit, but matched in mouth like bells,
> Each under each. A cry more tuneable

Was never hallowed to nor cheered with horn
In Crete, in Sparta, nor in Thessaly.
Judge when you hear.   [iv i 122–6]

Shakespeare seems to be varying Theseus's tone in the interests of character: this pragmatic country duke may be admitting that his dogs, though a fine pack, aren't necessarily perfect. It is entirely in keeping with his personality as a whole that he should do that, for his speeches frequently shift in tone, often for ironical effect. There is another example at the end of the speech. 'Judge when you hear', he says. After the tremendous build-up we expect to hear the barking of the dogs themselves; but instead his tone changes, for he has seen the lovers asleep on the ground, and a note of wry irony creeps in: 'But soft, what nymphs are these?'

Shakespeare took over Theseus's mocking sense of humour, especially at the expense of lovers' behaviour, from Chaucer's *The Knight's Tale*. When Chaucer's Theseus interrupts two friends, Palamon and Arcite, fighting to the death over Emelye, the lady they both love, he points out the absurdity of their situation:

The god of love, a, *benedicite*!
How myghty and how greet a lord is he! . . .
Now looketh, is nat that an heigh folye?
Who may been a fool, but if he love?
Bihoold, for Goddes sake that sit above,
Se how they blede! be they noght wel arrayed?
Thus hath hir lord, the god of love, ypayed
Hir wages and hir fees for hir servyse!
                    (lines 1785–1803, *Works*, ed. F. N. Robinson, 1957, p. 34.)

Shakespeare's Theseus speaks in a similarly ironical tone when he comes across the lovers lying asleep in each other's arms in the middle of a wood and draws what appears to be the obvious conclusion about what they have been doing out there:

Good morrow, friends – Saint Valentine is past!
Begin these woodbirds but to couple now?   [iv i 138–9]

The irony, and the varied tone, are both characteristic of

Theseus's speeches. In the opening scene, for instance, he shifts between orthodoxy and irony as he tries to persuade Hermia to accept her father's will by painting a sharply miserable picture of the alternative, a nun's existence. He asks Hermia if she

> can *endure* the livery of a nun,
> For aye to be in shady cloister *mewed*,
> To live a *barren* sister all your life,
> Chanting *faint* hymns to the *cold fruitless* moon.   [i i 70–3; my italics]

In the next line, he makes a rapid shift to a more respectably orthodox view – 'Thrice blessèd they that master so their blood' – but he soon switches back to lend his unmistakable support to the positiveness of love and marriage, expressed by another image from the natural world:

> But earthlier happier is the rose distilled
> Than that which, withering on the virgin thorn,
> Grows, lives, and dies in single blessedness.   [i i 74–8]

The last two lines emphasise how Theseus's manner varies from line to line. As the representative of orthodoxy, he must refer to the nun's chastity as 'single *blessedness*'; it *is* a blessed state; but the *image* he uses reveals unmistakably where his real sympathies lie, since what it stresses is not blessedness but barrenness: the nun's chastity is likened to a rose '*withering* on the virgin thorn'. Shakespeare compresses a great deal of variety and irony into Theseus's speeches.

The irony is important in providing a perspective on the extravagance and absurdity of the young lovers' behaviour. At the start of the final scene, especially, Theseus equates the 'seething brains' of lovers, who see 'Helen's beauty in a brow of Egypt', with those of madmen, and mockingly associates their irrationality with belief in 'fairy toys' [v i 2–11]. His scepticism is, however, counteracted by Hippolyta:

> But all the story of the night told over,
> And all their minds transfigured so together,
> More witnesseth than fancy's images,
> And grows to something of great constancy;
> But howsoever, strange and admirable.   [v i 23–7]

These lines are usually taken to mean that the lovers' minds
were all changed ('transfigured') so as to bear witness to something more than fanciful imaginings ('fancy's images') because
all their stories show consistency ('constancy'). But the words
'transfigured', 'fancy' and 'constancy' imply much more than
this. 'Transfigured', especially, has powerful overtones. When
Christ was transfigured, he was not simply changed, but
revealed in his essence, his divinity. Chaucer uses the word in
this sense of a divinity manifesting itself in *The Knight's Tale*,
when Palamon first sees Emelye and is so overwhelmed with
love that he assumes she must be Venus, the goddess of love,
revealing herself in human form:

> Venus, if it be thy wil
> Yow in this gardyn thus to transfigure
> Bifore me, sorweful, wrecched creature   . . .
>
>   (1104–6, Robinson, p. 28.)

Similarly, 'transfigured' in Hippolyta's speech suggests that
the lovers have been through an experience which has not
merely altered, but clarified, their emotions and feelings for
each other. 'Transfigured' implies something far more
powerful than simply 'changed'. It suggests a revelation of the
true nature of the lovers' minds and affections.

'Transfigured' occurs nowhere else in Shakespeare's work;
but 'fancy' and 'constancy' occur frequently, especially in connection with lovers' experience. John Dover Wilson usefully
describes the implications of 'fancy',

> by which Shakespeare and his contemporaries understood both
> what we now call sentimentality and, as the word still signifies, a
> passing inclination or whim. Originally a contraction of *fantasy*, the
> meaning of 'illusion', 'error', or 'unreality' yet clung to it, especially
> when the word was used in connection with Love. *A Midsummer
> Night's Dream*, for instance, is a dramatic essay on the theme of
> Fancy, with its tricks and deceptions. . . . Fancy, then, is not true
> love; it [does not] spring . . . from the heart. It is engendered in the
> eyes; it feeds upon mere appearances; it has no roots in reality, but
> dies almost as soon as it is born.
>
> (*Shakespeare's Happy Comedies*, 1962, p. 100.)

This is very relevant to the play as a whole, and especially to the lovers' experiences in the wood. The word 'fancy' constantly recurs in the play, in the sense that Dover Wilson explains: Helena is 'fancy-sick' [III ii 96] and follows Demetrius 'in fancy' [IV i 162], whereas the imperial votaress is 'fancy-free' [II i 164]. If Shakespeare uses 'fancy' to suggest deluded love, he often uses 'constancy' to mean true love, enduring affection. In *The Two Gentlemen of Verona* [II ii 8], Proteus offers Julia his hand in token of 'my true constancy'; and in *The Phoenix and the Turtle* (line 22), the two birds are symbols of 'Love and constancy'. Hippolyta means much more than that the lovers' experiences are consistent. Her language implies that they have moved from illusions and infatuations ('fancy's images') to a lasting affection ('something of great constancy'). The lovers' story shows this working out in practice.

4 THE LOVERS

Dover Wilson emphasises that 'fancy' is 'engendered in the eyes; it feeds upon mere appearances'. This is why the fairies' squeezing of the love juice on to people's *eyes* to make them fall in love is so appropriate an image of human infatuation. The action of the play draws attention to the dangers and confusions which result when lovers dote on outward appearances – and not only under fairy influence. Before the play starts, Demetrius has switched his affections from Helena to Hermia just as abruptly and illogically as he does later under the spell of the magic juice in the hectic confusions in the wood. Helena knows that love does not depend on mere appearances –

> Love looks not with the eyes, but with the mind,
> And therefore is winged Cupid painted blind. [I i 234–5]

– and that Demetrius 'errs, doting on Hermia's eyes'; but she has enough self-awareness to realise that she herself dotes on him for the same reason: 'So I, admiring of his qualities' [1 i 230–1].

Shakespeare gently mocks the extravagances and absurdities of young lovers, especially in the conventional language which they use to express conventional, and often deluded, sentiments: oaths, conceits, comparisons. Just how little lovers' vows may be worth is demonstrated in Helena's account of Demetrius's behaviour:

> For ere Demetrius looked on Hermia's eyne
> He hailed down oaths that he was only mine,
> And when this hail some heat from Hermia felt,
> So he dissolved, and showers of oaths did melt.   [1 i 242–5]

Although Demetrius provides an extreme example of conventional behaviour, and where it leads, the others are not essentially different. Egeus's attack on Lysander at the start presents a picture of a doting Elizabethan lover:

> Thou hast by moonlight at her window sung
> With feigning voice verses of feigning love,
> And stolen the impression of her fantasy
> With bracelets of thy hair, rings, gauds, conceits,
> . . .   [1 i 30–3]

And when Hermia vows to meet Lysander in the wood, she uses a series of standard comparisons to classical figures associated with love, the divine Cupid and Venus, and the mortal Dido and Aeneas, two star-crossed lovers such as Hermia and Lysander take themselves to be:

> I swear to thee by Cupid's strongest bow,
> By his best arrow with the golden head,
> By the simplicity of Venus' doves,
> . . .
> And by that fire which burned the Carthage queen
> When the false Trojan under sail was seen –
> . . .   [1 i 169–74]

In swearing by these classical figures, Hermia underlines the point that they see themselves as following the traditional path of lovers ('true lovers have been ever crossed') and that this 'trial' is as much 'due to love' as the rest of the conventional behaviour expected of lovers: 'thoughts, and dreams, and sighs, / Wishes, and tears – poor fancy's followers' [i i 150–5].

Shakespeare's presentation of the lovers is both humorous and sympathetic, as is made clear by the language he gives them. Often they speak with the lyrical ease I mentioned earlier. Even Hermia's classical catalogue of vows quoted above has a fluency about it which ensures that we do not lose patience with her conventional protestations. Later, however, Shakespeare exaggerates this style for humorous effects. Much Elizabethan love poetry is based on the technique of hyperbole, in which the poet provides a list of elaborate comparisons to express the beloved's beauty, or the intensity of his own feelings. Used skilfully, as Shakespeare himself uses hyperbole in his Sonnets, the technique can be very effective; but it degenerated too easily into empty formulae, mere cliché, a conventional style for conventional emotions. This style forms the basis of the lovers' language. Helena is not without charm and some shrewdness, but she keeps falling into the postures and phrases of the abandoned lover:

> I am your spaniel; and, Demetrius,
> The more you beat me I will fawn on you.
> Use me but as your spaniel: spurn me, strike me.   [ii i 203–5]

When Shakespeare in his own Sonnet 112 says to his lover 'You are my all the world', the hyperbole has a compressed directness which sounds a convincing expression of feeling; but when he gives a similar hyperbole to Helena, he pushes it into parody by expanding it in a quibbling and mechanical way:

> Nor doth this wood lack worlds of company,
> For you in my respect are all the world.
> Then how can it be said I am alone
> When all the world is here to look on me?   [ii i 223–6]

As the lovers fall under the spell of the magic flower, Shakespeare accentuates the rhymes of their chinking couplets to match their exaggerated language and to reinforce its humour. Thus, Helena and Lysander:

HEL.   Lysander, if you live, good sir, awake!
LYS.   And run through fire I will for thy sweet sake! [II ii 108–9]

Demetrius, similarly enchanted, even outdoes Lysander in extreme compliments:

O Helen, goddess, nymph, perfect, divine –
To what, my love, shall I compare thine eyne?
Crystal is muddy! O, how ripe in show
Thy lips – those kissing cherries – tempting grow!
That pure congealèd white, high Taurus' snow,
Fanned with the eastern wind, turns to a crow
When thou holdest up thy hand. O, let me kiss
This princess of pure white, this seal of bliss!   [III ii 137–44]

This is the perfect example of the conventional technique of exaggerated comparison. Helena is not merely a woman, but a goddess. She is perfect. Beside her, clear crystal is muddy. As so often in Elizabethan love poetry, the lady is compared to aspects of the natural world – her lips are cherries, the whiteness of her hand makes snow look as black as a crow – but the comparisons are rapidly trotted out like a series of automatic formulae, quite unlike the concrete evocations of the natural world with which Shakespeare presents the fairies' world or Theseus's hunt. This is Elizabethan artifice used for humorous effect, an effect intensified by the emphasis on the rhymes, even on rhymes within the lines: 'divine . . . thine eyne'. For the men's dispraise of Hermia, Shakespeare turns this technique upside down, so that the conventional catalogue of flattering comparisons to the beauty of the natural world becomes a vigorously insulting catalogue of comparisons to the more down-to-earth aspects of nature:

Get you gone, you dwarf,
You minimus of hindering knot-grass made,
You bead, you acorn!   [III ii 328–30]

Shakespeare expresses the mounting confusions of the scene with a feather-light mockery, accusations whipping rapidly backwards and forwards, emphasised by the rhymes of the couplets:

DEM. I say I love thee more than he can do.
LYS. If thou say so, withdraw, and prove it too.   [III ii 254–5]

In the case of Helena, however, Shakespeare achieves something more individual, developing the combination of shrewdness and sentimentality with which he characterised her in the
first scene. He expresses her sentimentality in a long, maudlin
recollection of schooldays with Hermia, beginning

> We, Hermia, like two artificial gods
> Have with our needles created both one flower,
> Both on one sampler, sitting on one cushion,
> Both warbling of one song, both in one key,   [III ii 203–6]

and continuing in this vein for another eight lines. But gradually Helena begins to enjoy the situation of being pursued by
both men, and she proceeds to expose the hollowness of their
extravagant speeches. First, she ironically lists Demetrius's
compliments – 'goddess, nymph, divine and rare, / Precious,
celestial' [III ii 226–7] – in order to blame Hermia for having set
him on to mock her with them. Then she switches from her
saccharine recollections of their schooldays to a much less
nostalgic view: 'She was a vixen when she went to school' [III ii
324].

After this extended humorous treatment of lovers' confusions, Shakespeare gives them a completely contrasting style,
simple and direct, to express their new feelings after they have
been properly paired by Oberon. Demetrius, the only member
of the quartet who has been permanently influenced by
Oberon's power, uses this new style first and most effectively. He
does not know 'by what power' his love for Hermia is 'melted as
the snow', but he finds that he loves Helena, not just with his
eyes, but with his heart:

> And all the faith, the virtue of my heart,
> The object and the pleasure of mine eye,
> Is only Helena.   [IV i 163–70]

Oberon's power has restored his original affection for Helena;
and Demetrius's final lines, which specifically mention the

healthy and the natural, remind us that Oberon's power itself derives from healthy, natural sources:

> as in *health* come to my *natural* taste,
> Now I do wish it, love it, long for it,
> And will for ever more be true to it.   [IV i 173–5]

Demetrius resumes this tone of wondering simplicity when the quartet is left alone:

> These things seem small and undistinguishable,
> Like far-off mountains turnèd into clouds.

Helena, appropriately, takes up his tone:

> And I have found Demetrius, like a jewel,
> Mine own and not mine own.   [IV i 186–91]

These quiet statements of amazement and affection, set against their earlier extravagance (their 'fancies'), perfectly suggest that sense of 'something of great constancy' which they have achieved under Oberon's benevolent influence.

5   The Mechanicals, and the Fusion of the Four Worlds

As the lovers leave the wood, Bottom awakes. Like them, he is confused; but whereas they express their feelings in simple, lucid verse, his characteristically colloquial prose cannot (or does not) actually articulate what he remembers:

> Methought I was – there is no man can tell what. Methought I was – and methought I had – but man is but a patched fool if he will offer to say what methought I had.

And his confusion is delightfully expressed in a speech which gets the various senses jumbled up:

> The eye of man hath not heard, the ear of man hath not seen, man's

hand is not able to taste, his tongue to conceive, nor his heart to
report what my dream was!   [IV i 205–11]

The joke here is that Shakespeare (or Bottom) is misquoting a
famous biblical passage, I Corinthians 2, verse 9: 'The eye hath
not seen, and the ear hath not heard, neither have entered into
the heart of man, the things which God hath prepared for them
that love him' (Bishops' Bible). Unlike the lovers, Bottom's
mind has not be 'transfigured' by his experience. It is abso-
lutely typical of him that he should not be daunted by this, and
that he should moreover see a way of turning his adventure to
specifically theatrical advantage: 'I will get Peter Quince to
write a ballad of this dream . . . and I will sing it in the latter
end of a play before the Duke' [IV i 211–14].

The mechanicals are, of course, particularly sharply dif-
ferentiated from the other three groups both by the broad
humour with which Shakespeare presents them, and by the
prose he gives them to speak. This colloquial prose characterises six individuals. These are human beings, not merely
clowns. They are determined to present their play as convincingly as they can; and as performance makes clear, the more
seriously they take themselves, the funnier they are. From the
start, Quince and Bottom are continuously set against one
another, a harassed director trying to control an irrepressible
leading actor who is confident that he can tackle any part.
Shakespeare gives Bottom a patiently condescending,
explanatory style which is exploited again in the play scene:
'First, good Peter Quince, say what the play treats on; then
read the names of the actors; and so grow to a point' [I ii 8–10].
Bottom demonstrates his prowess at playing tyrants, heroines
and lions, until Quince has finally had enough and slaps him
down: 'You can play no part but Pyramus.' In performance,
this usually leads to a production crisis as Bottom takes
umbrage and refuses to play any more, so that Quince has to
resort to wheedling diplomacy to lure him back to the job: 'for
Pyramus is a sweet-faced man; a proper man as one shall see in
a summer's day; a most lovely, gentlemanlike man. Therefore
you must needs play Pyramus.' This crescendo of compliments
works: 'Well, I will undertake it' [I ii 79–83].

Quince has his problems, too, with the rest of his cast.

No one seems able to pronounce 'Ninus', and Flute has other problems, as Quince's exasperated colloquial rhythms here show: ' "Ninus' tomb", man! – Why, you must not speak that yet. That you answer to Pyramus. You speak all your part at once, cues and all' [III i 91–3]. The personalities of the others are also sharply, economically expressed by their colloquialisms. Flute, cast as Thisbe because of his youth, is embarrassed – 'let not me play a woman' – and asserts his masculinity with some wishful thinking: 'I have a beard *coming*' [I ii 43–4]. Snug is captured in one speech: 'Have you the lion's part written? Pray you, if it be, give it me; for I am slow of study' [I ii 62–3]. Unlike Bottom, to whose theatrical ingenuity all things are possible, Snout is the kind of actor who thinks that nothing will work, a prophet of doom: 'By'r lakin, a parlous fear!' – 'Will not the ladies be afeard of the lion?' – 'You can never bring in a wall' [III i 12, 25, 59]. Starveling, unable to proceed with his performance in the play scene because of the heckling of the audience, finally loses patience altogether, abandons the doggerel verse he is supposed to speak, and resorts to forthright prose to call a thorn bush a thorn bush: 'All that I have to say is to tell you that the lantern is the moon, I the man i' th' moon, this thorn bush my thorn bush, and this dog my dog' [v i 250–2].

Shakespeare brings the mechanicals into contact with the other worlds in two particularly effective scenes, one half-way through the play, the other at the end. Bottom's meeting with Titania in III i is the climax of the first half of the play. Shakespeare has skilfully manipulated the plots to prepare for their meeting and to ensure that it has the maximum humorous effect. In II ii Oberon anoints Titania's eyes with the love juice as she lies asleep in her bower. The audience then become so absorbed in the humorous confusions of Lysander's wooing of Helena and of the mechanicals' rehearsal that, by the time Bottom in his ass's head begins to sing, they have completely forgotten about Titania asleep upstage. So when, in the midst of his singing, they suddenly hear her superbly judged line, 'What *angel* wakes me from my flowery bed?' [III i 122], it comes as a complete surprise and yet also seems quite inevitable, the perfect crowning absurdity of the scene, as the fairy queen falls in love with the braying ass-headed weaver. The stage situation itself is another image of the irrationality of doting on outward

appearances: 'mine *eye* [is] enthrallèd to thy *shape*' [III i 132].
Bottom explicitly makes the point: 'Methinks, mistress, you
should have little reason for that. And yet, to say the truth,
reason and love keep little company together nowadays' [III i
135–7]. This homespun wisdom, while it spells out a major
concern of the play, is also very characteristic of Bottom's
individual style, just as, in beautifully incongruous contrast,
Titania's lyricism is typical of the fluent authority of her language:

> I am a spirit of no common rate.
> The summer still doth tend upon my state.   [III i 145–6]

Those superb lines, especially the second, emphasise her
authority over the natural world, and when she instructs her
fairies to attend on Bottom, she once more evokes the inhabitants of that world:

> The honey bags steal from the humble bees,
> And for night-tapers crop their waxen thighs
> And light them at the fiery glow-worms' eyes
> To have my love to bed and to arise.   [III i 163–6]

This speech combines lyrical beauty with the delicate humour
that Shakespeare always applies to Titania's diminutive attendants, as if the fairies were engaged in mock-heroic adventures
in stealing honey bags, and running dangerous risks lighting
their tapers from 'fiery' glow-worms.

A notable aspect of the characterisation of Bottom is that he
is never at a loss in any situation, however unexpected. After an
initial moment of alarm at Titania's adoration, Bottom is soon
giving her the benefit of his observations on reason and love as if
she were one of his fellow-actors, and expansively joking with
the fairies – so much so, in fact, that Titania has to shut him up
at the end of the scene. As she leads him to her bower, she fears
that another downpour is imminent – 'the moon methinks looks
with a *watery* eye' – and suggests that the bad weather is
nature's sympathetic response to the trials of lovers:

> And when she weeps, weeps every little flower,
> Lamenting some enforcèd chastity.   [III i 193–5]

Presumably Bottom responds with the start of a new speech, or more likely, as in most productions, with an ass's bray, provoking Titania's firm instruction: 'Tie up my lover's tongue, bring him *silently*.' This delightful incident beautifully crowns a brilliant scene which, by combining two of the four worlds and their contrasting styles, provides a very effective conclusion to the first half of the play. At the end, an equivalent scene brings together all four worlds.

The play scene is the logical climax of the narrative. This is the wedding night not only of Theseus and Hippolyta, which has been anticipated from the start, but of the four lovers also; and it is the big night for Bottom and his company. The plot of the mechanicals' play obviously parodies the lovers' adventures: this, without the benevolent intervention of Oberon, is how they might have ended up. 'Pyramus and Thisbe' (much funnier, of course, in performance than in reading) exaggerates the style both of tragic and quasi-tragic love-stories and of Elizabethan love poetry. Take, for instance, Pyramus's address to Night:

> O grim-looked night, O night with hue so black,
> O night which ever art when day is not!
> O night, O night, alack, alack, alack.   [v i 167–9]

This sounds irresistibly like a parody of a curious passage in Shakespeare's tragedy of star-crossed lovers, *Romeo and Juliet*. Thinking Juliet dead, her Nurse cries out:

> O woe! O woeful, woeful, woeful day!
> Most lamentable day, most woeful day
> That ever, ever, I did yet behold!
> O day! O day! O day! O hateful day!
> Never was seen so black a day as this.   [*R. & J.* iv v 49–53]

Unfortunately, we do not know whether *A Midsummer Night's Dream* was written just before or just after *Romeo and Juliet*, but this odd scene with its clumsy repetitions verges on the farcical. It is possible that Shakespeare came to think so too, and turned its deficiences to good use as a real farce, changing the repetitions of 'O day' to 'O night', and crashingly stating the obvious with 'O night which ever art when day is not'.

This is necessarily conjectural; what is quite certain is that Bottom's address to the Wall –

> And thou, O wall, O sweet, O lovely wall,
> That standest between her father's ground and mine,
> Thou wall, O wall, O sweet and lovely wall,
> Show me thy chink to blink through with mine eyne   [v i 171–4]

– with its clanging rhymes and lumbering verse lines, is an overt parody of Golding's translation of the Pyramus and Thisbe episode in Ovid's *Metamorphoses*. Golding's verse (Book iv 91–3) reads almost like a parody in itself:

> 'O thou envious wall', they said, 'why let'st thou lovers thus?
> What matter were it if that thou permitted both of us
> In arms each other to embrace? . . .'

And Thisbe's lament for the dead Pyramus parodies conventional Elizabethan compliments (like Demetrius's comparing Helena's lips with 'kissing cherries' [iii ii 139–40]) by grotesquely mis-applying them: 'These lily lips, / This cherry nose, / These yellow cowslip cheeks' [v i 322–4]. Although mis-applied, these compliments and other moments in 'Pyramus and Thisbe' (the 'mine/eyne' rhymes, for instance, and Pyramus's and Thisbe's use of classical figures, however confusedly, for their vows of love) are too close to the lovers' own expressions and experiences for their own comfort – which is no doubt one reason why they heckle the play so persistently.

Theseus, however, takes a different view. His typical wry irony reappears in response to the description of 'Pyramus and Thisbe' as a 'tedious brief scene', 'very tragical mirth':

> Merry and tragical? Tedious and brief?
> . . .
> How shall we find the concord of this discord?   [v i 56–60]

Although, with his sense of humour, Theseus can share the joke with the lovers, he himself makes a major contribution to the way in which the whole scene makes 'concord of this discord' in the courteous, considerate way he treats the actors:

> Our sport shall be to take what they mistake;
> And what poor duty cannot do, noble respect
> Takes it in might, not merit.   [v i 90–2]

When Hippolyta says 'I am aweary of this moon. Would he
would change', Theseus replies with characteristic humour, 'It
appears by his small light of discretion that he is in the wane'.
He can see the joke, but he can also see that they must 'in
courtesy' give the actors a hearing [v i 244–7]. In this way,
Theseus achieves a relationship between the mechanicals and
their audience, and particularly between himself and Bottom:

> Love, therefore, and tongue-tied simplicity
> In least speak most, to my capacity.   [v i 104–5]

Not that Bottom is tongue-tied: after he has turned from prais-
ing Wall to cursing him, Theseus jokes that 'The wall,
methinks, being sensible, should curse again' – whereupon
Bottom immediately switches off his characterisation of
Pyramus to make things clear to him:

> No, in truth sir, he should not. 'Deceiving me' is Thisbe's cue. She
> is to enter now, and I am to spy her through the wall. You shall see –
> it will fall pat as I told you.   [v i 179–84]

The patiently explanatory tone of this is very funny, as the star
actor takes the trouble to explain the mysteries of his art to the
uninitiated; but it also establishes a sense of communication
between Bottom and Theseus, achieved because Theseus
makes the effort to enter the world of the play, and Bottom to
break out from it in order to clarify points for him. This delightful moment is very typical of Shakespearean comedy: it uses
humour to express a human relationship, just as there was
communication, as well as incongruity, between Bottom and
Titania earlier.

These moments of relationship *across* the different plots help
to give the scene, and the play as a whole, its increasing sense of
concord growing out of discord. Such moments increase as the
scene nears its end. Hippolyta, who has been so scornful about
the play, eventually admits that 'the moon shines with a good

grace', and even, as Bottom intensifies Pyramus's grief, 'Be-shrew my heart, but I pity the man' [v i 259–60, 282]. Faced with the possibility of an epilogue, Theseus hastily tells them that 'your play needs no excuse. Never excuse'. He gives his ironic humour rein: 'if he that writ it had played Pyramus and hanged himself in Thisbe's garter, it would have been a fine tragedy'. Then, realising the offence his tactlessness must be causing, he quickly makes amends: 'And so it is, truly, and very notably discharged' [v i 346–51]. As midnight strikes, his remark ''tis almost fairy time' must have its touch of sly irony in view of his earlier mockery of 'fairy toys'; and in one of the play's most inspired moments, the fairies confound his scepticism about their existence by invading his own palace in order to bless it.

This is the most powerful and satisfying image of concord in the play, finally uniting all four plots in one scene, and it emphasises the fairies' benevolence in the last moments of the play. Oberon and Titania themselves, now that they are 'new in amity', will bless Theseus and Hippolyta, their ex-lovers, over whom they earlier quarrelled so bitterly. It is another characteristic of Shakespearean comedy that the final harmony is not imperilled by a clear recognition of past discord:

> To the best bride bed will we,
> Which by us shall blessèd be.   [v i 393–4]

Oberon also promises that the other lovers, whose affairs he put to rights, shall 'Ever true in loving be' [v i 398]. His influence ensures lasting love. 'And the blots of nature's hand', those evils which the malevolent spirits of tradition were often supposed to cause (mole, harelip, birthmark) will be kept at bay by these fairies. But significantly Nature's blots will be warded off by Nature's own means: it is typical of Shakespeare's entire presentation of these fairies that they should bless the birde-beds not with exotic incense but with consecrated 'field dew' [v i 405]. Theseus's palace is granted 'sweet peace' by creatures that 'Hop as light as bird from briar' [v i 384].

PART TWO: PERFORMANCE

6 INTRODUCTION

A review of Peter Hall's production of *A Midsummer Night's Dream* at Stratford-upon-Avon in 1959 began: 'After a century or so of plain sailing in the calm waters of the grand old Mendelssohn bosky dell tradition, producing *A Midsummer Night's Dream* has become a problem again' (*Leamington Spa Courier*, 5 June 1959). The problem was to find an alternative to the traditional approach which had prevailed for 'a century or so'. This approach is usefully characterised in T. C. Kemp's account of Michael Benthall's 1949 Stratford production. He found it

> magnificent in detail, but short in rustic enchantment. James Bailey's rich Veronese palace, the sumptuous Renaissance-Greek costumes, the bevies of tulle-draped ballerinas, the black-garbed cohort that attended Oberon, the trunk-tortured depths of the forest and the spangled starlight of the Athenian night, all these made for theatrical opulence rich and rare.
>
> (*The Stratford Festival*, 1953, p. 234.)

He thought, however, that all this opulence overwhelmed the magic rather than enhancing it. 'We felt that we were in the neighbourhood of Olympus rather than . . . somewhere in the Arden of old Warwickshire' where the fairies inhabit 'any spinney between Stratford and Kenilworth'. In short, the *scale* of the production was inappropriate.

Most directors in the past thirty years have reacted against the nineteenth-century traditions preserved in a production like this. In particular, they have attempted many different ways of presenting the fairy world. At Stratford, where the play has received more major productions than anywhere else, George Devine in 1954 interpreted them in terms of the animal world: Puck was a mixture of ape and hedgehog, while the other

fairies were birds, with Oberon plumed like a peacock and
Titania wearing broad white eye-streaks like a falcon. Patrick
Stewart's Oberon, directed by John Barton in 1977, was a
strikingly impressive mixture of a dark-skinned prince 'from
the farthest steep of India' [II i 69] and a pastoral god 'playing
on pipes of corn' [II i 67]. In Ron Daniels's 1981 production,
Titania's attendant fairies were sinister puppets manipulated
by black-clad actors, through whom Oberon had to fight his
way to Titania's bower.

Sometimes the court has been clearly contrasted with the
fairy world. George Devine's bird-fairies were sharply dis-
tinguished from what Richard David called 'the Assyrian
sumptuousness of Theseus and his court', as well as from the
other worlds, so that 'the action plainly moved on four levels'
(*Shakespeare Survey*, 8, 1955, p. 138). John Barton set Patrick
Stewart's dark, exotic Oberon against a sturdily Elizabethan
court, largely dressed in white, but he also reconciled court and
countryside in his simple set: the formal patterned wooden floor
of the court was surrounded by the trees of the wood. Some
directors have related the two worlds even further, to the point
of doubling Oberon with Theseus and Titania with Hippolyta.
Something of a modern tradition has been established here.
The reasons for it, and the problems it raises, will be considered
later.

There are two other modern stage traditions which have
become almost universally accepted. Most directors have
emphasised the absurdity of the young lovers, and have also
realised that the humorous stage business which naturally
accumulates around the mechanicals is most effective when it
arises from character and situation, rather than from externally
imposed gags. Richard David makes the interesting point that
when the mechanicals are faithful 'to themselves (and so to
Shakespeare) . . . their . . . funniest moments [can be]
unscripted', and he gives an example from George Devine's
production: 'When the difficulty of introducing moonshine into
their theatre first strikes them, their mute consternation, sustained without a blink by all six actors through minutes of
vociferous applause from the audience, gave us the men themselves' (p. 137). This also makes it clear that an audience's
enjoyment is not diminished but increased when the mechani-

cals take the problems of rehearsing and performing their play with full seriousness, as in the 1981 Stratford production, where the mechanicals were dismayed at Quince's suggestion that they should learn their parts 'by tomorrow night' [I ii 93].

This particular production, by Ron Daniels, took the general reaction against nineteenth-century conventions to a new extreme by putting those conventions to ironical use and parading their artificiality. Theseus's red and gold Victorian throne-room was emphatically one-dimensional, painted on to flats. The wood scenes took place, not even in front of a Victorian representation of a wood, but on the deserted stage of a Victorian theatre at night, strewn with theatrical properties, including scenic flats with their wooden frames, not their painted sides, facing the audience. For some people, this ironical display of nineteenth-century artifice was confusing: there appeared to be no obvious point of contact between a deserted Victorian theatre and a moonlit wood. Others simply ignored the irony, and enjoyed the performance out of a sense of nostalgia for traditional nineteenth-century stagings of the *Dream*.

The mock-Victorian approach, and the varying audience reaction to it, made two useful points about the attitude of modern directors towards the interpretation of *A Midsummer Night's Dream*. First, the discrepancy between Shakespeare's wood and Daniels's Victorian stage raises the question of how far the staging of the play should reflect the style in which it is written. This question is of central relevance to the discussion which follows. Second, the production provided a reminder that the traditional nineteenth-century associations of the *Dream* still seem sufficiently alive for most modern directors to react against them to a greater or lesser extent. A detailed consideration of the very different ways in which four directors have done this not only illustrates more fully some of the interpretations of the four worlds of the play mentioned so far, but also indicates the variety of possible approaches to *A Midsummer Night's Dream* in performance.

7 PETER HALL'S PRODUCTIONS

The Play, Royal Shakespeare Company, 1959–69; Britten's Opera, Glyndebourne, 1981

The modern director who has returned to the play most frequently is Peter Hall. A tentative experiment at Stratford in 1959 led to very successful revivals at Stratford in 1962 and at the Aldwych Theatre in London in 1963, and then to a film released in 1969. Peter Hall said that each production was 'a development of previous knowledge' (*Sunday Times*, 26 Jan. 1969). In 1981 he directed Benjamin Britten's operatic version at Glyndebourne. Britten re-created the essence of the *Dream* in musical terms with such astonishing success that Peter Hall's work on the opera was at the same time the latest stage in his developing interpretation of Shakespeare's play.

Peter Hall's aim in the RSC production of the play in 1959 was 'to take *The Dream* back to its beginnings, perhaps for a wedding in an Elizabethan country house'. This was an attempt to establish the correct proportions and scale of the play. The set suggested the rush-strewn great hall of an Elizabethan manor house, dominated by a minstrels' gallery reached by two large staircases from the front of the stage; between these, under the gallery, was an inner stage. At gallery level, bridges led off-stage to left and right, and a formal Elizabethan façade painted on gauze disappeared when back-lit to reveal the trees and bushes of the wood in soft, misty light, on the upper level; these were supplemented at ground level by further bushes in tubs; Titania's bower was revealed behind the curtains of the inner stage. In this way, the transformation to the wood was rapidly and convincingly achieved without ever entirely losing the atmosphere of the manor house; and this exactly caught the blend of court and countryside central to the play. (See Plate 1.)

A similar blend was achieved by less elaborately architectural means in the Aldwych revival of 1963, when the staircases and balcony were replaced by a large empty hall in warm red Elizabethan brick. The entire wood was moved into this hall on a platform, complete with a large tree and flowering bushes; the rushes which had strewn the floor in the earlier version now formed a screen for Titania's bower. So whereas previously the fairies had to enter the wood on the upper level before coming down the staircases to play their scenes on the main stage, this revision achieved a much more concentrated effect by enabling the wood to occupy the whole centre of the stage; but behind it, the enclosing walls of the manor house could always be dimly seen, so that the combination of court and country came over even more strongly than before.

At Glyndebourne, for the 1981 opera production, this basic principle remained. The proscenium arch was framed by the beams of the hall, and red brick walls and huge Elizabethan casement windows were lowered in for the play scene. Britten begins his opera not at court but in the wood, responding to Shakespeare's poetic realisation of it by making it a living presence, expressed in orchestral sighs and breaths marked 'slowly animating'. Peter Hall accordingly had bushes, trees, branches and logs animated by black-clad actors so that the wood moved mysteriously in the moonlight, re-forming for different scenes and finally sliding away with the departure of the fairies in the dawn light. It is typical of Britten's re-creation of the play that, while he does not actually set Oberon's sunrise speech, he completely captures its effect in the string phrases preceding and accompanying Oberon's reconciliation with Titania [cf. IV i 70–91], which express the brilliant clarity of early morning, of the sun's 'fair blessèd beams'. Peter Hall responded magnificently to this: a huge sun rose gradually from the back of the raked floor, as if from the horizon, reflected in the floor's shiny perspex surface, which had earlier suggested the waterlogged conditions of Titania's account. It is perhaps ironical that no production of the play itself has captured the transformation from 'watery' moonlight to glorious sunrise as well as this staging of the opera. A major drawback of Peter Hall's film version was that it over-emphasised the mud and rain which the text describes, at the expense of the natural beauty and radiance which it also describes. The film did, however, maintain the country house atmosphere of the stage versions, since it was made in the hall, park and wood of a real country house, Compton Verney in Warwickshire.

In the theatre, the country house setting enabled Peter Hall to anchor each of the play's levels 'to reality', as Irving Wardle said of 1963 revival, and especially to provide an unusually rounded interpretation of Theseus as a pragmatic 'country Duke':

> The opening scene at Theseus's court . . . acquires a life of its own, exploiting to the full Theseus's pre-nuptial frustration and his embarrassment in the Egeus affair. The portrait of wry, magnanimous nobility Tony Steedman gives in this . . . part typifies the integrity of the production.
>
> (*The Times*, 14 June 1963.)

This interpretation broke new ground in demonstrating that Theseus's lines are much subtler and more varied in tone than they appear in many productions. My analysis of Theseus's speeches in Part One is very much indebted to it. While Peter Hall's appreciation of irony and humour helped to give substance to Theseus and his court, it also led him in 1959 to over-stress the absurdity of the young lovers, who were played for broad, boisterous, often farcical humour different in degree rather than in kind from the humour of the mechanicals. This, of course, emphasised the link between 'Pyramus and Thisbe' and the adventures of the lovers in the wood, but it missed the more important contrast between the lovers' extravagant Elizabethan conceits and the simple directness of their language when they awake.

It was in his presentation of the lovers that Peter Hall's interpretation of the play developed most significantly over the years. The broader humour was toned down, enabling Diana Rigg to give a subtly detailed performance as Helena in 1962, 1963 and in the film. She certainly made the most of the absurdities of the part: the attitudinising of 'Stay, though thou *kill* me, sweet Demetrius' [ii ii 90] and the deep-throated, mock-tragic inflection at '*de-e-eath* or absence soon shall remedy' [iii ii 244]. She was not, however, *simply* absurd: she *used* humour in the interests of character in the delighted, flattered smile that flickered across her face at the first impassioned declarations from Lysander and Demetrius; and her warm, flexible delivery of the lines ranged from parody and indignation to a sisterly affection for Hermia and finally to a tenderness which caught beautifully the lyrical simplicity of 'And I have found Demetrius, like a jewel, / Mine own and not mine own' [IV i 190–1].

Even so, it was not until he staged the opera version at Glyndebourne that Peter Hall realised the full potential of all four lovers. They were subtle, eloquent and passionate, without any loss of humour. Dale Duesing's Demetrius made a tremendous comic climax out of his enchanted awakening: 'O Helen, goddess, nymph, perfect, divine' [III ii 137]. Felicity Lott's Helena managed a delicious transition from the velvet glove in her recollection of schooldays with Hermia to the claw within as she turned on Hermia to call her a vixen and, fatally, a 'puppet'. As Hermia responded to this with increasing but tensely contained rage, she was beautifully supported by the varied reactions of the other three, developing from amusement to nervousness to genuine alarm. In capturing precisely that combination of mockery and human sympathy which is at the heart of both Britten's and Shakespeare's presentation of the four lovers, this quartet gave the best performances of the characters that I have seen anywhere.

If the Elizabethan country house setting provided a convincing context for Theseus and his court, it did so to an even greater extent for the fairies. Oberon and Titania wore splendid Elizabethan court clothes, but the misty fabric of which these were made also suggested the cobwebs, dew and gossamer of the wood. They had bare feet, pointed ears and bushy grey wigs. At Glyndebourne, Oberon's wig – brushed back at the sides like huge wings – was streaked with black down the centre like a badger. This suggestion of an animal, combined with the single earring and ruffed collar of an Elizabethan grandee, exactly reflected the way in which Shakespeare has drawn on both court and countryside to create the fairies. Puck was an urchin, and the attendant fairies combined doublets and helmets with pixies' ears: they were fairy guardsmen, snapping to attention or bowing elaborately to Bottom. There was nothing remote or balletic or ethereal about these fairies. Peter Hall says that he has 'always tried . . . to make them earthy, so that they're more sensual than the mortals' (*Films and Filming*, Sept. 1969), and he has never been afraid to give them very specific, often humorous, stage business, especially Puck. At Stratford in 1959 and 1962, and in the film, Ian Holm panted eagerly like a dog and sniffed on scenting the presence of mortals; he blew the fog out of his mouth; he put the men to sleep with a snap of his fingers, the girls with a kiss. At Glyndebourne, Damien Nash shook every last drop of magic juice into Lysander's eyes, and vigorously swept the floor and re-set the furniture in the last scene.

In such ways, Irving Wardle observed, the fairy world 'escape[d] bloodless disembodiment', particularly Ian Richardson's interpretation of Oberon: 'His appearance, as a gilded Elizabethan fop, and his habit of direct address ("I am invisible", with a mocking bow to the audience) in no way interfere with his exquisitely formal delivery of the enchanted poetry' (14 June 1963). This Oberon could switch easily from a mocking 'I wonder if Titania be awaked' [III ii 1], with an ironic eye on the audience, to the almost studied beauty with which he delivered Oberon's account of Titania's bower [II i 249–56], his vision of the imperial votaress [II i 148–68], and his sunrise speech [III ii 388–93]. These were spoken directly to the audience from positions very close to them. All this enhanced, rather than detracted from, the sense of a fairy world at such moments, for the very simple reason that it corresponded to the way Shakespeare has written the speeches. The direct communication with the audience and the unethereal staging matched the immediate, concrete language with which Shakespeare evokes the countryside in order to present the fairies.

These features even more strongly characterised Judi Dench's Titania at Stratford in 1962. It is a measure of the way in which Peter Hall developed his interpretation that, whereas Titania's long speech 'These are the forgeries of jealousy' [II i 81–117] had been drastically cut in 1959, it was given in full at the first revival in 1962, and thereafter. Judi Dench's performance prompted several reviewers to comment that the speech had much more cogency than in most productions. In placing such emphasis on the rural world of which Titania is a part, Peter Hall provided the actress with a real context in which she could convey a sense of her involvement with that world: the characteristic little catch in her voice expressed both her genuine concern that 'The ox hath therefore stretched his yoke *in vain*' [II i 93] and her sympathy with the 'human mortals' who 'want their winter cheer' [101]. This sympathetic response to the rural world built to a great climax as she dwelt lingeringly upon the way the seasons '*change* / Their wonted liveries' [112–3], before she broke the mood with a sharp reminder to Oberon that the two of them have been responsible for all this chaos.

It was disappointing that the film version upset the balance between the rural and the courtly, which had been so securely achieved in the theatre, by turning the fairies into naked goat-haired satyrs. Judi Dench summarises the problem. Although Titania was presented 'nearly naked', 'I didn't feel nearly as "sensual" as I did in that formal, cobwebby, stiff costume that Lila de Nobili designed' for the stage version (quoted in David Addenbrooke, *The Royal Shakespeare Company*, 1974, p. 117). She makes some valuable points here. She clearly does not feel that Elizabethan court costumes need be restrictive. This one actually helped her to convey the role's 'sensual' quality, its combination of the courtly and the rural, at once 'formal' and 'cobwebby', as she puts it. Depriving Titania and Oberon of their court clothes in the film also robbed them of their courtly dimension. Even so, the film did succeed in finding a striking visual equivalent for Titania's close relationship with the natural world, using a close-up technique for the 'forgeries of jealousy' speech so that Judi Dench's face was set against constantly changing images of seasonal chaos. At the reference to 'the moon, the governess of floods' [II i 103], she and Oberon glanced upwards together, their faces caught by the moon-beams. This Titania also kept a wary weather eye on the 'watery' moon later, as she led Bottom to her bower [III i 193]; and the film did at least have the advantage of demonstrating in close detail the sheer variety which made her such an outstanding Titania.

Judi Dench has the full range of qualities which Titania requires: natural authority, a spontaneous impish sense of humour, and the ability to speak formal verse with both clarity and sensuous beauty. All these various elements were combined in her two scenes with Bottom. She was particularly successful in communicating that mixture of sensuousness and

absurdity both in her infatuated falling in love ('So is mine eye
enthrallèd to thy shape' [III i 132]), and in her instructions to the
fairies. Here, her tone could be mock-heroic ('the *fiery* glow-
worms'), or conspiratorial ('The honey bags *steal* from the
humble bees'), or it could be lyrical, humorous and infatuated,
all at the same time:

> And pluck the wings from painted butterflies
> To fan the moonbeams from his sleeping eyes.   [III i 163–8]

She used her irresistible sense of humour both in delivering the
lines and in her chuckling response to Bottom's wit and wisdom; but she could move from that to instant authority at 'I am
a spirit of no common rate' [III i 145] and as she commanded her
fairies to tie up Bottom's tongue to prevent any more of his ass's
brays interrupting her. She also demonstrated a delicious combination of sensuality and delicacy as she stroked his 'fair large
ears' later [IV i 4]. (See Plate 3.)

In the film and in the opera at Glyndebourne, Bottom wore
an ass's head with movable ears and mouth; but at Stratford,
although he had ass's hooves on his hands and feet, he only
wore 'fair large ears', not a complete head. This had the advantage of allowing his facial expressions full play and of emphasising how Bottom remains very much himself during these scenes
– especially when Paul Hardwick played the part, 'quietly
discovering unexpected truths about life, as when he accepts
modestly but with respectful rapture the embraces of Titania
and the homage of her fairy attendants' (*The Times*, 18 April
1962). This performance matched the emphasis on the warm
humanity of the mechanicals in general. Their scenes were
played very slowly, not only because they were slow on the
uptake, but also to suggest that they were thinking things out.
They took their play very seriously, and were determined to
work out all its problems so as to present it as effectively as
possible. Both these points were demonstrated in the film at the
moment when Snout, who had been assiduously following the
script during the rehearsal, glanced down at it in bewilderment
to discover why Pyramus should need an ass's head, before
realising that Bottom himself was 'changed' [III i 108]. In the
play scene, all the mechanicals took their roles with a deter-

mined seriousness which made the scene funnier still. Their humanity extended across the plots as well, establishing a relationship between Bottom and Theseus:

> Bottom stands triumphant and flushed. In his ecstasy he drops his ludicrous wooden sword; it lies between him and Theseus. There is a pause. The duke bends, picks it up, . . . and, with a bow, presents it to Bottom. Their eyes meet for a moment. In that moment there is a 'gentle concord in the world'.
>
> (Gareth Lloyd Evans, *Shakespeare*, II, 1969, p. 85.)

This sense of concord was greatly assisted by the intimacy of the setting in the 'Great Chamber' of a country house, with the Lord of the Manor making a genuine effort, without sacrificing his sense of humour, to enter the play world of his tenants; and that concord grew stronger still after the play and bergomask were over.

In the earlier versions, the various couples departed across the bridges that led offstage from the gallery, pausing on them to bid each other goodnight. When they were gone, the central trapdoor was flung up and Puck appeared. The fairies suddenly materialised from everywhere, and lit their tapers at the glowing 'wasted brands' of the brazier left over from the play scene. Oberon liberally distributed a shower of glitter dust which represented the consecrated field dew, and the fairies processed up the stairs and through the house to bless the sleepers with it. Oberon and Titania paused to kiss on the bridge that led to the 'best bride bed' of Theseus and Hippolyta, a fitting image of their harmony on their way to bless their former lovers. While some of the details varied subsequently, the essence of this treatment remained throughout all Peter Hall's versions. What was especially effective about the 1981 opera production at Glyndebourne, was that the fairies could be seen gathering outside the casement windows before entering through them. This gave a powerful sense of a country house surrounded by a wood and its inhabitants, a final image of the harmonious combination of court and countryside upon which Peter Hall's interpretation has been based from its tentative start in 1959 to its full, confident flowering in 1981. Since his approach reached straight to the heart of the play, Peter Hall has been, for me, its most illuminating modern interpreter.

8 PETER BROOK'S PRODUCTION

Royal Shakespeare Company, 1970–73

Irving Wardle spoke for the majority of reviewers when he said that the 1963 revival of Peter Hall's *Dream* had 'a richness of detail and emotional depth that force one to encounter the play as if for the first time'. He spoke for an even greater majority in hailing Peter Brook's Stratford version seven years later as 'a masterpiece' (*The Times*, 28 Aug. 1970); but because the production was so radical, it aroused fierce opposition as well as great enthusiasm.

Peter Brook aimed to find 'the hidden play behind the text' by turning 'to the art of the circus and the acrobat because they both make purely theatrical statements. We've worked through a language of acrobatics to find a new approach to a magic that we know cannot be reached by 19th-century conventions' (quoted in the *Daily Telegraph*, 14 Sept. 1970). The set consisted of three white walls surrounded by steel ladders and a cat-walk, from which members of the cast could watch scenes in which they did not appear. Wearing shapeless, brightly coloured costumes which suggested oriental acrobats or circus clowns, the fairies used the props of the circus or the gymnasium – trapezes, swings, ropes – to 'fly' in and out of this white box.

Titania's bower was a huge scarlet ostrich feather suspended high above the stage; for the lullaby 'You spotted snakes', this was lowered to a mid-air position, and surrounded by four playground swings suspended at different levels but linked together, on which the four fairies sat in oriental squatting positions, arms raised with palms outwards to ward off danger. (See Plate 4.) Puck confused the duellists by striding above their heads on stilts. The only visual concession to the fact that Shakespeare has set the play in a wood took the form of coils of wire suspended from fishing rods on the cat-walk. These vaguely suggested trees, but much more often they constituted obstacles in which the lovers became entangled, especially Hermia at the end of II ii: as she fled from them through the auditorium, the fairies sent these coils swirling out over the heads of the audience in sinister pursuit.

These four hefty, sinister fairies and the vicious wire coils were representative of a strong element in the production. John Kane, who played Puck and who wrote a detailed account of rehearsals for the Royal Shakespeare Company's newspaper *Flourish*, described how at one early run-through, the fairies 'were certainly mischievous if not downright malevolent. The forest and its inhabitants exuded a primitive savagery that infected everyone that came in contact with them' (*Flourish*, II, 7, 1971). This sinister element was reflected in the set. If it suggested a circus or a gymnasium, its steel staircases and observation platform equally strongly suggested a prison, an externalising of what Brook called the 'darkness' in the minds of Theseus and Hippolyta during their public encounters. The play, he said,

> unfolds like a dream before their wedding in which an almost identical couple appear – Oberon and Titania. . . . The couples are so closely related that we felt that Oberon and Titania could easily be sitting inside the minds of Theseus and Hippolyta.
> (*Plays and Players*, Oct. 1970.)

So the two couples were played by the same actors, in order to suggest that the events in the wood represented the dark animal fantasies beneath the public front which Theseus and Hippolyta present to the world, in which Theseus/Oberon has Hippolyta/Titania raped 'by the crudest sex machine he can find', by an animal 'that couldn't carry the least sense of romantic attachment. Oberon's deliberate cool intention is to degrade Titania as a woman'.

This interpretation provided the first half of the production with a tremendous climax, in more senses than one. John Kane described how Brook 'carefully prepared the ground' in rehearsal:

> While the dialogue between . . . Bottom and Titania proceeded, Peter surreptitiously motioned Ben [Kingsley] to begin playing [his guitar]. Sara [Kestelman] heard the soft chords and as she reached the lines, 'Be kind and courteous to this gentleman', began to sing the words to a melody that took shape even as we listened to it. . . . The [fairies] suddenly joined in with an unrehearsed but perfect four-part harmony backing to Sara's song; and then from all round the room, the rest of the company added their contributions.

1. *Peter Hall's RSC production, Stratford, 1959.* Theseus's country house transformed into the wood, with Titania's bower under the balcony. Photograph: Holte Photographics.

2. *Peter Hall's Glyndebourne Festival Opera production, 1981.* Cynthia Buchan as Hermia, Ryland Davies as Lysander, Dale Duesing as Demetrius and Felicity Lott as Helena. Photograph: Guy Gravett.

5. *Robin Phillips's production, Stratford, Ontario, 1977.* Maggie Smith as Hippolyta. Note the deliberate resemblance to Elizabeth I. Maggie Smith doubled Hippolyta with Titania. Photograph: Zoë Dominic.

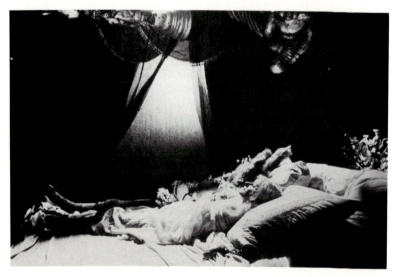

6. *Elijah Moshinsky's production, BBC TV, 1981.* Titania's bower: Brian Glover as Bottom, Helen Mirren as Titania. BBC copyright photograph.

Titania's 'Be kind and courteous' speech-song was re-positioned to follow the dialogue between Bottom and the fairies, and her line 'To have my love to bed and to arise' was repeated at the end of the song, with 'arise' interpreted in such a way that the song could lead directly into a wild orgasmic conclusion. The fairies hoisted Bottom on to their shoulders; one of them thrust a muscular arm up between Bottom's legs like a grotesque phallus; Oberon swung on a rope across the stage, and the rest of the cast threw paper plates and streamers like confetti over Bottom and Titania as the Mendelssohn Wedding March blared out. This sequence had its roots in the first run-through, as John Kane reported:

> a wild gaiety seized the company. . . . we whipped the play along
> . . . until it eventually exploded during the Titania/Bottom con-
> frontation in a welter of torn newspaper, moaning cardboard phal-
> luses and Felix Mendelssohn. As the noise and laughter died away,
> we looked around the room and as though awakening from a dream
> we realised that we had been possessed by some wild anarchic
> force . . . . We had brushed momentarily against Peter's 'secret
> play' . . . . Unseen by us, Peter carefully prepared the ground for
> these 'revelations'.

This 'wild gaiety' certainly infected the audience, who responded with cheers and applause. Irving Wardle spoke of the 'thrill of the unexpected' in finding the scene played as 'an occasion for real sexual revels' (*The Times*, 28 Aug. 1970).

But while Peter Brook had manipulated the apparently improvising actors to reveal his own 'hidden play', his handling of the scene raises the important question of how successful he was in interpreting Shakespeare's text. On this point, the critics were sharply divided. Helen Dawson felt that 'the play and its poetry leap into almost Oriental clarity' (*Observer*, 30 Aug. 1970); yet John Russell Brown said that 'movement and noise obliterate speech, or make so strong a counter claim for the audience's interest that words can scarcely be followed' (*Shakespeare Survey*, 24, 1971, p. 132). The treatment of Titania's speeches in this scene was a test case.

As she fell in love with Bottom, she lay on her back and

curled her legs around his, clawing at his thighs, gasping and
gabbling in sexual frenzy as she said:

> And I do love thee. Therefore go with me.
> I'll give thee fairies to attend on thee,
> And they shall fetch thee jewels from the deep,
> And sing while thou on pressèd flowers dost sleep;   [III i 147–50]

– whereupon Bottom jumped on top of her. Jan Kott might
have been describing this staging when he wrote, three years
earlier, that Bottom is the lover Titania 'wanted and dreamed
of' because in 'the Renaissance the ass was credited with . . . the
longest and hardest phallus. . . . The monstrous ass is being
raped by the poetic Titania, while she still keeps on chattering
about flowers' (*Shakespeare Our Contemporary*, revised edition,
1967, p. 183). Jan Kott's and Peter Brook's attitudes to
Shakespeare's text closely correspond. Kott's dismissive
phrase 'chattering about flowers' clearly implies that the language which Shakespeare gives to Titania is of no account and
can simply be disregarded. The text itself does not matter to
him, only what Brook calls the 'hidden play *behind* the text'. But
of course the dramatic point which Shakespeare is making
depends upon his very precise use of language, upon the humorous contrast between the formal lyrical verse with which
Titania declares her love for Bottom, and the colloquially
self-important prose with which he responds to it. The lyrical
beauty of Titania's speeches was completely thrown away in
this performance's frenzied gabbling and gasping; Shakespeare's characterisation of Bottom, too, was obscured in the
way that he was presented.

Whereas Peter Hall had limited Bottom's transformation to
ass's ears and hooves to help him preserve his humanity and
individuality, in Peter Brook's version the tiny pointed ears
which were fitted to Bottom's cloth cap, the black button nose
which suggested Mickey Mouse, and the clogs on which he
crashed around the stage, reduced him to a grotesque, slaver-
ing monster. Yet Brook claimed that he saw the mechanicals
not as comic butts but as human beings who 'believe in [their
play] passionately' (quoted in *The Times*, 29 Aug. 1970). Peter
Hall achieved precisely this effect in his versions; but in the first

mechanicals' scene in Brook's production, Bottom addressed 'A very good piece of work, I assure you' [i ii 13], not to his fellow-actors, but to the audience, like a music-hall comedian; and at a later revival, Bottom's list of alternative beards [i ii 86–9] was turned into a song in which Bottom and the musicians marched up and down the theatre aisles. Richard Peaslee, the composer, reported that Brook 'felt the scene needed a lift. It was partially a theatrical instinct to goose the action a bit with a musical number . . . right out of the old musical halls' (Authorised Acting Edition of Peter Brook's production, 1974, p. 71). This seems at complete odds with Brook's professed aim to take the mechanicals seriously as human beings rehearsing a play.

On the other hand, he took the play scene *so* seriously that Shakespeare's own humorous effects were sacrificed altogether. I have never known 'Pyramus and Thisbe' get fewer laughs. The reason was not simply that the mechanicals took themselves seriously (all good performers of these parts do that), but that Brook staged the entire final scene so as to demonstrate his own theatrical theory: 'the actor's art is truly celebrated in this episode – it becomes a mysterious interplay of invisible elements, the joy, the magic of the *Dream*' (*Plays and Players*, Oct. 1970). This theory led him to iron out the distinctions between the different groups of characters. Instead of heckling the mechanicals' play, the lovers participated in it: Thisbe's promise to meet Pyramus at Ninus' tomb – 'Tide life, tide death, I come without delay' [v i 200] – was turned into a vocal ensemble sung not only by Flute, Bottom and Snout (as Wall) but by the lovers too. Brook's 'mysterious interplay of invisible elements' also involved breaking down the distinctions between stage and audience. Oberon's final instruction to the fairies 'Meet me all by break of day' [v i 412] was altered to 'Meet *we* all by break of day' and addressed directly to the audience. Instead of blessing the palace, the whole cast left the stage and bounded up the theatre aisles to shake hands with the audience.

The staging of both these episodes reflected Brook's belief that 'it is wrong to direct the *Dream* as if the fairies, the aristocrats and the mechanicals belonged to . . . different worlds' (quoted in *The Times*, 29 Aug. 1970). The trouble with this view is that it completely disregards the structure of the play.

Shakespeare certainly brings the four separate worlds into a final harmony, but he achieves this harmony not by playing down the differences between the various worlds, but by exploiting them. He establishes the individual characteristics of each group in the first place, so that when he brings them together, he can play upon the audience's awareness of the differences at the same time. The mechanicals' play parodies the lovers' experiences, so the lovers heckle it. To unite mechanicals and lovers in a harmonious musical ensemble is to contradict the way in which Shakespeare has written the scene. The fairies' blessing of the palace is not a generalised 'celebration of the theatre', but a very precise, and very satisfying, conclusion to the events of the play. The piquancy of the dramatic situation here, as the fairies bless the marriage bed of their mortal ex-lovers, is inevitably lost if they are the same people. Because Brook had deliberately blurred Shakespeare's own distinctions between four sharply characterised worlds, he had to substitute his own kind of harmony, in which the actors shook hands with the audience, for Shakespeare's.

Some people felt that, by freeing the audience's imagination from such literal encumbrances as trees and flowers, the production concentrated attention both on the words of the text and on the processes of magic. Sally Jacobs, the designer, represented this point of view:

> We were . . . absolutely certain that to be able to get that beautiful shock of catching your breath, we couldn't produce the magic in the way that it has always been produced. . . . There's no such thing as the Magic Flower. . . . It's not magic: we know it's only a prop. So what to replace such objects with? . . . We remembered the spinning plates from the Chinese Circus – the whirling plate on the stick works very well for the Flower.
>
> (Acting Edition, pp. 47–8.)

So during Oberon's vision of the imperial votaress which introduces the flower, two trapezes were lowered to the stage floor, arriving in time for Puck to go in search of the flower by putting 'a girdle round about the earth' on one of them [II i 160–76]. When Puck subsequently gave the 'flower' to Oberon, he spun a plate from a plastic rod, and Oberon caught it on another rod, both on trapezes in mid-air. Their trapezes were then lowered to the ground during Oberon's speech about Titania's bower [II i 247–54].

This sequence certainly succeeded in making the audience 'catch their breath', but not in focusing their attention on Shakespeare's text. Quite the contrary. Alan Howard spoke Oberon's lines with great clarity, but the slow descent of the trapezes inevitably distracted completely from what he was saying, both in the bower speech and in his explanation of how the flower gained its power of bestowing love. The flower is not 'only a prop', but a prop which the language invests with very special significance for the action of the play. In any case, spinning plates and trapezes are 'only props' as well, and ostentatiously alien to anything mentioned in Shakespeare's very specific text at this point. As so often in this production, it was impossible to reconcile what was said with how it was presented. Of course, a director must bring out the essential meaning of a play, but that meaning cannot be arbitrarily separated from the style and language in which the play is written. The wood, the wild flowers, the combined court and rural worlds are essential features of *A Midsummer Night's Dream*. They are not merely the decorative surface of a 'hidden play' but the very means by which Shakespeare creates his fairy world. In dispensing with them entirely, Peter Brook inevitably jettisoned not merely stale theatrical conventions, but the essence of Shakespeare's play as well.

A useful perspective on the production's achievement is provided by Robert Cushman, looking back on it after twelve years: 'it looked lovely and was fun, especially the juggling, but those who claimed that it redefined the play can never have read or seen it. The lovers are *always* played young and comic, the clowns are usually funnier and therefore richer; and . . . the acting was nothing special' (*Observer*, 28 March 1982). At the time, its admirers spoke as if the only theatrical alternative to plates and trapezes was nineteenth-century tradition; but in the very next major production, at Stratford, Ontario, in 1976–77, Robin Phillips achieved a *Dream* just as original as Brook's by basing it on the style and subject matter of those very speeches that Brook so completely disregarded.

9   ROBIN PHILLIPS'S PRODUCTION

Stratford, Ontario, 1976–77

Robin Phillips took as his starting-point Oberon's vision of the imperial votaress [II i 148–68] and the play's other specific associations with Queen Elizabeth I. He placed Elizabeth herself at the centre of the play, interpreting Titania and Hippolyta, played by the same actress (Maggie Smith), as aspects of the Queen's personality. The whole play became, as it were, a dream of Queen Elizabeth's. (See Plate 5.)

Accordingly, Robin Phillips set the play in Elizabeth's palace. It is not difficult to suggest Elizabethan associations on this particular stage, because the Festival Theatre at Stratford, Ontario, is modelled on the basic principles of the Elizabethan theatre. Its central acting area is a huge platform which juts right out into the audience. At the back of this platform, steps lead to exit doors on both sides of the stage, and further steps to an upper level, supported by pillars. When it is empty, this vast stage can suggest great isolation, both emotional and physical – as at the start of this production, when Hippolyta stood alone and spot-lit, while a female voice sang Bottom's line 'I have had a most rare vision' [IV i 203] in the distance. She was the perfect image of Elizabeth in her red wig, with its ringlets and jewels, and in her magnificent black and gold costume.

The open Ontario stage can, however, also give a sense of great activity and ceremony, once it is filled with actors and props. When the general stage lighting came up, Hippolyta was surrounded protectively by an entourage of court ladies whose costumes and wigs resembled her own, and opposed by Theseus and a huge array of Elizabethan gallants. The whole stage was a dazzling vision of black and gold Elizabethan court splendour. Great branched candlesticks evoked the atmosphere of an Elizabethan long gallery. Later, an exceptionally imaginative lighting system which shed shafts of light like will o' the wisps, together with giant white flowers, suggested the wood, but always within the context of an Elizabethan palace.

Theseus, at least in the 1977 revival which I saw, played down the subtle irony of his lines in order to present a stern, humourless threat of male domination: this, the production implied, was how Elizabeth regarded the prospect of marriage, which for personal and political reasons she avoided all her life. But she might entertain very different fantasies about *lovers* in the amorous atmosphere of a court where she was the object of flattering praise and adoration from afar; and such fantasies formed the basis for the central forest sequence in which she took on the persona of Titania, Theseus that of Oberon, and Philostrate – played as a devoted old courtier (perhaps Elizabeth's chief minister Burghley) – that of Puck. Since Hermia and Helena, like the court ladies, presented further images of Elizabeth in their formal clothes and red wigs, the lovers' confusions suggested that this might be Elizabeth's own view of the follies of love. Peaseblossom, Cobweb, Moth and Mustardseed were played by members of Theseus's entourage, so that Titania's bower was guarded by young courtiers like the 'pensioners' who guarded Elizabeth herself, exactly the kind of sensuous youths about whom Elizabeth might have had hot dreams. In this context, Titania's remark about the flowers in the wood 'lamenting some enforcèd chastity' [III i 195] seemed to take on an additional layer of meaning: the flowers might be sympathising not only with someone who has been forcibly robbed of her chastity, but also with someone who has been compelled to preserve it, the 'enforcèd chastity', in this second sense, of Elizabeth herself.

Several other passages also appeared in a new light, especially when the action returned from the wood to the court for the final scene. Hippolyta's face froze in half-recollection at Demetrius's line 'one lion may, when many asses do' [v i 152] and again at Theseus's remark that Bottom 'might yet recover, and prove an ass' [302–3]. Puck's line 'from the presence of the *sun*' [375] referred to Hippolyta/Elizabeth, and as Oberon spoke of 'the issue there create' [395], Hippolyta's hand moved instinctively to her childless womb. It was almost inevitable, in presenting the play as Elizabeth's dream, that Theseus's speech about imagination [v i 2–22] should be given to Hippolyta/Elizabeth, who also spoke Hippolyta's own lines which present the other side of the case [23–7]. But the crucial phrases 'transfigured so together' and 'something of great constancy' were played down, with Hippolyta turned evasively away from the audience, perhaps to suggest that, while Elizabeth could entertain fantasies about the lunacy of love, she could not accept its transfiguring power. Whatever the reason, the deliberate throwing away of this crucial speech indicated the limitations of the interpretation. So did the elaborately contrived staging of certain episodes.

To enable Oberon and Titania to change back into their Theseus/Hippolyta clothes for the hunt scene in IV i, for instance, the passage beginning 'Come, my Queen, take hands with me' [84–101] had to be pre-recorded and relayed over speakers, while the courtiers performed a mating dance under the giant white flowers which suggested the wood. The blessing of the palace was also relayed, to allow Hippolyta to be alone on stage as at the start, except for Puck/Philostrate to speak the epilogue. The treatment of both episodes emphasises that, whatever the motivation for doubling Hippolyta/Titania and Theseus/Oberon, it will inevitably involve some awkward contrivance in performance, for the simple practical reason that the exit of one pair is followed without any kind of break by the entry of the other pair at IV i 101. The doubling also weakens the structure of the play, with its counterpointing of four distinct worlds.

However, in this production, the loss of structural variety involved in the doubling was almost compensated for by the variety of personality and delivery which Maggie Smith brought to her double (or triple) role as Titania/Hippolyta/Elizabeth. This was especially noticeable in her outstanding treatment of Titania's meeting with Bottom, which ended the first half of the production. Here Maggie Smith proved fully equal to the range of Shakespeare's writing for Titania in this scene. She had an effortless authority which stopped Bottom dead in his tracks with a single word ('OUT of this wood do not desire to go!') and which really made you believe that the summer tended upon *her* state [III i 143–6]. She brought an exquisite blend of verbal beauty and her own very personal sense of humour to the 'humble bees' passage [III i 159–69]. She herself was 'a most rare vision', bathed in moonlight; her shimmering dress and flowing hair gave the impression that she felt liberated from the restrictions of the formal court clothes she wore as Hippolyta. When she finally embraced Bottom, this seemed the inevitable climax towards which both the scene and the first half of the play had been moving, prepared for by Robin Phillips's interpretation and by Maggie Smith's authority, radiance and humour, which gave genuine enchantment to the whole episode.

But such an original interpretation of the play depends upon performers of this quality if it is to convince. Both her performance and the production as a whole were hampered because neither Bottom nor Theseus/Oberon was played by an actor of similar calibre. When Jeremy Brett played Theseus/Oberon opposite Jessica Tandy the year before in the first showing of this production at Stratford, his performance, impetuous and imperious, reminded reviewers of Elizabeth's favourites Leicester and Essex. If it had been possible for him to partner Maggie Smith in the revival, the tension between Theseus and Hippolyta in the opening scene, and the quarrel between Oberon and Titania, might have had greater effect, and the inherent disadvantages of doubling the roles might have been diminished still further. As it was, Theseus/Oberon was merely adequate, and Bottom much less than that. Indeed, the mechanicals in general provided an object lesson in how these parts should *not* be played: they completely lacked humanity, substituting funny voices and externally imposed, self-conscious jokes for characterisation. And since the interpretation of the court scenes was so sophisticated, there could be no harmonious mingling of different levels of society in the play scene: instead of contrasting with the court and the lovers within the play, these 'funny men' seemed to have strayed in from another play – and indeed from another, inferior, theatrical world altogether.

That this impression was a consequence of the weakness of particular performers rather than of the director's interpretation was made clear by the stylish humour he encouraged elsewhere. Maggie Smith's perfectly timed, irresistibly wicked throwaway delivery of Hippolyta's 'This is the silliest stuff that ever I heard' [v i 207] won the biggest laugh of the evening, but its witty sophistication devastatingly exposed the ineptitude, not merely of the mechanicals, but of the actors who played them. By contrast, the lovers' scenes communicated the absurdities of young love with complete success, and Martha

Henry's Helena was a brilliantly funny *tour-de-force*. Her performance rivalled Maggie Smith's in technical range, but not in effortless ease, for she brought a massive armoury of verbal and physical effects to bear on Helena's lines. The almost baroque elaboration of this performance of Helena was very much in keeping with that of the production as a whole.

In its elaboration, and in its radical approach, this was obviously not a production to emphasise the simpler pleasures of the play. It had weaknesses among the performers and in the contrivance of some aspects of the staging. What, then, was its particular contribution to the theatrical interpretation of the play? A good production need not slavishly follow every literal detail of the text, but there should be a demonstrable relationship between the style of the play and the way in which it is presented. The theatrical images created by Robin Phillips and his designer, Susan Benson, were not only stunningly beautiful in themselves, they also harmonised with a great deal of the most characteristic language. That first spot-lit image of Hippolyta as Elizabeth obviously guided the spectator's response in a specific direction. The sense of a brilliant Elizabethan court was so strong that, from the start, one was alerted to the way in which Shakespeare has written many central passages. The formal speeches of Titania and Oberon (especially, of course, the vision of Queen Elizabeth), and the hunt speeches of Theseus and Hippolyta, for instance, took on a heightened definition. The context established by the production made one especially aware of the kind of Elizabethan court ceremonial upon which Shakespeare seems to have drawn to create the special style of such passages.

It would, however, be most misleading to imply that this production was merely a pedantic journey in search of historical origins. It was an imaginative and exhilarating modern staging, whose achievement was to leave the impression, not only of the richness of the play, but also of the extent to which that richness depends upon the fact that the *Dream* is an Elizabethan play in a more precise sense than simply a play written in the last decade of Elizabeth's reign.

10   Elijah Moshinsky's Production

BBC Television, 1981

The programme for Robin Phillips's production called the play 'a modified version of the Masque'; and the masque was also an influence on the BBC television production in 1981, directed by Elijah Moshinsky, who had been responsible for a brilliant *All's Well That Ends Well* earlier in the same series. He had created the strong sense of a real society, which *All's Well* requires, by basing it visually on seventeenth-century paintings; and he made use of similar images to give his *Dream* a solid context.

At the start, the disputants in the Egeus scene sat at a table in a seventeenth-century library, Lysander and Demetrius wearing Stuart fashions rather than Elizabethan ones. The counter-pointing of the plots was instantly established in the second scene when Flute aped their fashions: a young Cavalier smoking a clay pipe. The most striking and specific example of the influence of seventeenth-century art on this production was Titania's bower, not a flowery bank but a bedchamber based on Rembrandt's picture *Danae*. This shows the naked Danae leaning forward in bed eagerly anticipating the arrival of her lover Jupiter, who appeared to her transformed into a shower of gold. The shower is not actually represented in the picture, but the golden tone suggests that the canopy over the bed, the bedclothes, the gilded Cupid above Danae's head, and Danae herself, are all touched by the glow of Jupiter's gold. Elijah Moshinsky used all these features for Titania's bedchamber, especially its glowing golden light, with Titania herself a clothed version of Danae. (See Plate 6.)

Whereas the use of paintings by Rembrandt and Vermeer established the society of *All's Well* and sustained it with absolute consistency, the greater variety of location required by the *Dream* led to more uneven results. Although Titania's bower was a bedroom, this did not mean that we were deprived of the wood, which was presented with a muddy, rain-swept realism which recalled Peter Hall's film. Puck and the fairies sported in a large forest pool which was central to the action throughout the entire middle section of the play. Unlike Peter Hall's film, however, this realism was set against a sky whose moon and clouds suggested a stage set. The vistas down which, for instance, Helena pursued Demetrius, in II ii, evoked the perspectives and landscapes of seventeenth-century masques. They also hinted at nineteenth-century settings. Elijah Moshinsky 'wanted a sort of romantic realism – an echo of the nineteenth-century approach without its top heaviness' (*A Midsummer Night's Dream*: BBC TV Shakespeare, 1981, p. 19).

His interpretation was rather low-key, serious, even sombre. When Lysander and Demetrius argued over Hermia, for instance, threat and counter-threat were spoken in hardly more than whispers, in obvious awe of a stern, inflexible Theseus; and when Hermia and Lysander planned to elope, they also spoke in secretive whispers, as if afraid of being overheard by court spies. Helena was oddly interpreted as a frowsy, bespectacled bluestocking. It wasn't surprising that Demetrius should have preferred Hermia; what was surprising was that he should have fallen for her in the first place. This unhappy figure, afraid of being left on the shelf, matched Helena's forsaken situation but not the lightweight language which she uses to express it. It was hard to believe that this gloomily studious Helena had ever listened to the song of the lark or noticed the hawthorn buds to which she refers so lyrically [I i 184–5]. This interpretation was an extreme indication of the prevailingly sombre tone, and the lack of gaiety and humour in this approach.

The approach was partly dictated by the medium. Since there is, of course, no possibility of audience reaction in televised Shakespeare, the director presented the mechanicals especially in ways that did not depend on such reaction. The presence among them of several actors from television situation comedies initially suggested that jokes might take precedence over character, but in fact these were the most serious interpretations of the parts I have seen, and three of them were interestingly original. Geoffrey Palmer's Quince was humourless, brisk and well-spoken, vividly recalling the sort of man one often finds running amateur dramatic societies – which is of course precisely what Quince is doing. In his prologue to 'Pyramus and Thisbe' [v i 108–17], he got the phrasing and punctuation right to start with, only garbling the later part of the speech out of stage fright: this actually helped to clarify the joke that Shakespeare is making in this speech. Even his verbal slip 'paramour' for 'paragon' (very credibly corrected by the aspiring young Cavalier of a Flute) arose less from ignorance than from distraction at losing his star actor [IV ii 11–14]. In their director/actor relationship, the temperaments of the two characters, surprisingly but convincingly, reversed the usual expectations: Brian Glover's Bottom was good-natured and not especially vainglorious, certainly not overbearing, while Quince grew increasingly impatient and bad-tempered at each of Bottom's suggestions, which threatened his authority – until, unexpectedly and effectively, he was delighted with Bottom's idea about the Wall, at which he and the rest of the cast broke into relieved laughter that at least one of their problems was solved. But when Bottom, not hamming his lines but attempting to be as expressive as possible, made his mistake 'the flowers of odious savours sweet', Quince derisively repeated 'odious!' before snappily correcting it to 'odours' [III i 75–6]. When John Fowler's Flute spoke out all his part at once, he did so stretched out on the ground in a mixture of coyness and sensuality as he prepared to play the female part with which he had been landed. These three performances were notably successful consequences of the serious approach.

So were the fairies, though here both the interpretation and the effect were less consistent. Peter McEnery's Oberon, arriving on a sinister black horse 'from the farthest steep of India', had long black hair which carried the faint suggestion of an Indian guru; in complete contrast, Helen Mirren was a ravishing golden-haired Titania. It was a good idea to have the changeling child present, as the cause of all the trouble, but a serious miscalculation to have Titania clutch him to her breast throughout the *whole* of the 'forgeries of jealousy' speech, his shuffling and whining completely distracting attention from what Titania was saying. She was surrounded by a flock of children, an entire fairy family (were they all changelings?), dressed like her in variants upon Stuart masque costume. Phil Daniels's Puck, on the other hand, was a paradoxical mixture of the human and the animal. He was a lean, wiry, half-naked faun yet he wore a ruff; he spoke like a rough diamond from London's East End yet he showed wolvish fangs, and at one evocative moment lapped up water from the forest pool like a fox; he panted excitedly at the thought of the magic herb's power and malevolently dragged Flute repeatedly through the pool in III i, yet at other times he expressed adolescent wonder as he fondled Hermia or tried on Lysander's glove.

This interpretation did not achieve its full effect, because Phil Daniels gabbled the verse; and a similar inability to speak verse undermined the lovers' scenes. After looking at her reflection in the forest pool, for instance, Helena said 'No. (*very decisively; pause:*) No. (*pause; then as a very flat statement:*) I am as ugly as a bear' [II ii 100]. This was the more noticeable because the Hermia of Pippa Guard (who had had the advantage of playing the part in John Barton's 1977 Stratford production), spoke with such clarity and musical beauty. In their quarrel scene, the lovers' speeches were overlapped, so that while Demetrius was pouring out his hyperbolical praises of Helena ('That pure congealèd white, high Taurus' snow'), she had already begun to accuse him of mocking her: 'O spite! O hell!' [III ii 141–5]. Here, the interpretation of Helena, which had seemed excessive at the start, began to work: she greeted Hermia with open arms, only to be disillusioned yet again when she felt Hermia was conspiring with the men to mock her. The strained, artificial rhetoric of her maudlin speech about their childhood innocence seemed to be just the terms which such a blue-stocking would use, especially her comparison of Hermia and herself to 'a double cherry, seeming parted / But yet an union in partition' [III ii 209–10]. This was greeted with admiring amusement by the two men, approving her forced ingenuity because they were in love with her; and her studious gloom gave way to rueful smiles as she felt that, after all, people could love her. The overlapping phrases and the fighting and squabbling in the middle of the forest pool certainly gave a vigorous, immediate impression of a quarrel, but at the expense of the lightweight humour of the scene.

The most successful aspect of these wood scenes was the way in which the fairies moved from potential (or actual) malevolence to harmony and reconciliation in their dealings with the lovers, with Bottom, and with each other. After the lovers' quarrel, for instance, Oberon repeatedly plunged Puck's head under water in the pool as a punishment – only to clutch him protectively in his arms during the sunrise speech a few lines later. During the following sequence, in which Puck puts the lovers to sleep, the resources of television were most fully and successfully exploited. Each shot caught Puck's faun-like body in a different pose. The first shot looked up at him from below, a grinning, almost demoniac, 'goblin', 'feared in field and town' [III ii 398–9]; the second image was a double one, showing both his fencing with Lysander and his reflection in the pool; next he appeared kneeling astride Lysander to put him to sleep, then patting a tearful Demetrius consolingly; the next shot showed his face at right angles to Helena's as he kissed her asleep; and by the final image he had progressed all the way from danger-ous goblin to 'sweet Puck' as he collected their cloaks and doublets and covered them as they slept.

With Bottom and Titania, the range was greater still. The transformation of so un-domineering, so good-natured a Bot-tom into an ass was, in keeping with the sombre emphasis of the interpretation, a more disturbing one than usual. The trans-formation itself gave him fluffy ears and hooves, but also elon-gated teeth, and streaks of fur across the face. Moreover, Bot-tom saw himself in the pool, so that he was aware of what was happening to him. This obviously gave additional edge to his later reluctance to talk about it ('Methought I was – and methought I had –' [IV i 206–7]). Possibly, though, the text suggests a less conscious, more instinctive awareness of change, so that a phrase like 'You see an ass head of your own, do you?' [III i 110–1] is unconscious irony. Titania's awakening was elaborately contrived: as we switched back from Bottom's rather woebegone figure isolated in the wood to her bed-chamber, the sound of his singing was accompanied by music so as to seem almost beautiful to her in her dream: a clever idea if somewhat at odds with the simple humour of the incongruity between fairy queen and braying weaver. Nevertheless, Helen Mirren struck a fine balance between the sensuality which is her chief characteristic as an actress and the formal beauty of her verse as she wooed him.

A balance between even greater extremes was achieved in their second scene [IV i], where Elijah Moshinsky at once ran his greatest risk and achieved his greatest success. He inter-preted Bottom's repeated instructions to the fairies to scratch him as a means of exciting him to orgasm, which was accompanied by a triumphant ass's bray. Here Moshinsky made the sexual implications of Titania's love for Bottom very explicit, but he immediately counterbalanced it with an amazing sense of harmony in Titania's reconciliation with Oberon; and he did so by fully exploiting the qualities of the Rembrandt picture on which the bedchamber was based. As Bottom fell asleep beside Titania, the camera closed in on her face, framed in golden hair, resting on the pillows in that glowing light. Then Puck's smiling face appeared above the back of her bed, looking down on her in the same way that Cupid looks down on Rembrandt's Danae. Oberon's face appeared to the left of the shot, which hardly altered during the rest of the episode, so that Oberon's, Titania's and Puck's faces were held in close-up. Oberon tenderly kissed the spell from her eyes, using 'Dian's bud' only to stroke her lips gently, implying that his restored love for her had more power to undo the 'hateful imperfection of her eyes' than any magic. When Titania woke she was convulsed with laughter at the idea of being enamoured of an ass, before her very tender reunion with Oberon. This episode moved from one extreme of grossness to the opposite extreme of tenderness, and it worked so well because it made the most of a basic principle of Shakespearean comedy: the sense of harmony is achieved most securely when balanced against contrasting discord. The sombreness, and in this scene the grossness, made the eventual reconciliation seem the sweeter by contrast.

The harmony achieved here was not, however, recaptured in the final scene. Much here, certainly, was admirable. The earlier approach to the mechanicals was successfully sustained. Bottom put as much eloquence into Pyramus's demise as into his protestations of love, and Flute played Thisbe with great intensity, heartbroken at kissing the wall's hole rather than Pyramus's lips. In his wig and dress, he looked a much more attractive heroine than, for instance, Helena. Here was a marvellous opportunity for exploiting the connections between the lovers' experiences and those of Pyramus and Thisbe. But the chance was missed because the staging was miscalculated. The setting was a banqueting-hall, with tapestries and screen; but a banqueting-table of enormous width completely cut off these actors from their stage audience, so we were hardly ever able to see the lovers' reactions, still less to see them in close proximity to the mechanicals, without changing shot. A more serious problem was that the Theseus was so one-dimensional that there was virtually no sense of his court world at all, and the mechanicals', lovers' and fairies' plots remained isolated strands instead of coming together in his palace.

This emphasised the hard way that, if one of the four worlds is ineffective, the total effect of the play is jeopardised. Even so, in its sombreness and its use of seventeenth-century art to evoke a Stuart, rather than an Elizabethan, court world, this production presented the *Dream* from an interestingly different viewpoint, and demonstrated yet another of the variety of approaches possible to this apparently inexhaustible play.

READING LIST

The most useful editions are: Stanley Wells (ed.), *A Midsummer Night's Dream* (New Penguin Shakespeare, 1967); and Norman Sanders (ed.), *A Midsummer Night's Dream* (The Macmillan Shakespeare, 1971).

Both provide a good deal of useful information very concisely. Either is preferable to the New Arden edition (1979); this buries the text beneath a vast mass of commentary, gives 'sources' a prior claim over stage history, and in general shows no awareness of theatrical considerations.

Also useful is the BBC TV Shakespeare edition (1981), with an Introduction by John Wilders. This edition contains interesting information about the making of the television version, has production annotations next to the text, and illustrations.

BACKGROUND

If more information is needed than Wells or Sanders provide, the following may be recommended:

Geoffrey Bullough, *Narrative and Dramatic Sources of Shakespeare*, 8 vols (Routledge: London, 1957–75): vol. 1, *Early Comedies, Poems, 'Romeo and Juliet'* (1957).

M. W. Latham, *The Elizabethan Fairies* (Columbia UP: New York, 1930; reprinted Octagon Books: New York, 1972).

K. M. Briggs, *The Anatomy of Puck* (Routledge: London, 1959).

C. L. Barber, *Shakespeare's Festive Comedy: A Study of Dramatic Form and Its Relation to Social Custom* (Princeton UP: N.J., 1959; reissued by Meridian Books: New York, 1963). This relates the play to pageants and festivals, both popular and aristocratic. It is less satisfactory in interpreting the play itself, as I have suggested in Part One.

LITERARY CRITICISM

Among the more useful accounts are:

Helen Gardner, 'As You Like It', in John Garrett (ed.), *More Talking of Shakespeare* (Longman: London, 1959); reprinted in subsequent collections including J. Russell Brown (ed.), *'Much Ado About Nothing' and 'As You Like It'* (Macmillan Casebook, 1979). Though Helen Gardner mentions the

Dream only incidentally, this is the best account of Shakespearean Comedy that exists.

G. K. Hunter, *William Shakespeare: The Later Comedies* (British Council 'Writers and their Works' series: Longman: London, 1962). This contains an excellent brief account of the *Dream*.

David P. Young, *Something of Great Constancy* (Yale UP: Newhaven, Conn., 1966). The chapter on the *Dream* is the principal account of the play as a study of imagination, and is discussed in my Introduction to Part One.

The field of criticism is usefully surveyed in:

D. J. Palmer, 'The Early Comedies', in Stanley Wells (ed.), *Shakespeare: Select Bibliographical Guides* (Oxford UP: London, 1973).

Antony Price (ed.), *A Midsummer Night's Dream* (Macmillan Casebook, 1983). This selection includes excerpts from some of the critical studies mentioned in this present list, e.g., M. W. Latham, C. L. Barber, G. K. Hunter, David P. Young.

PERFORMANCE

The productions mentioned only briefly at the start of Part Two are given detailed description in:

Richard David, 'Plays Pleasant and Unpleasant', *Shakespeare Survey*, 8 (Cambridge UP, 1955): volume editor A. Nicoll. This discusses George Devine's 1954 Stratford production, and is in general an article of exceptional interest by a leading modern critic of Shakespeare in performance.

Roger Warren, 'Comedies and Histories at Two Stratfords, 1977', *Shakespeare Survey*, 31 (Cambridge UP, 1978): volume editor K. Muir. This discusses John Barton's 1977 production at Stratford-upon-Avon.

Roger Warren, 'Interpretations of Shakespearean Comedy, 1981', *Shakespeare Survey*, 35 (Cambridge UP, 1982): volume editor Stanley Wells. This discusses Ron Daniels's 1981 production at Stratford-upon-Avon.

The two sides of the controversy over Peter Brook's 1970 production are represented by:

Peter Thomson, 'A Necessary Theatre' and J. Russell Brown, 'Free Shakespeare' – both in *Shakespeare Survey*, 24 (Cambridge UP, 1971): volume editor K. Muir.

INDEX OF NAMES